Legacy Unbroken

Dedication

To the love of my life, Rachel, thank you for being my partner through everything.

To my three daughters, Kathleen, Ava, Everly, and my granddaughter Scarlet: I want this book and the message within to be a reminder that there is always hope. For you, and for anyone who faces the darkness, know the light is always there.

For assistance with situations involving domestic abuse, please visit www.DisasterAssistance.gov or call 1–800–799–SAFE (7233).

If you or someone you know struggles with depression, or suicidal thoughts, please visit National Institute of Mental Health (www.nimh.nih.gov) or the Veterans Crisis Line (www.veteranscrisisline.net); for more immediate crisis, call or text 988.

Table of Contents

About the Author

Aaron Thornock is a 20-year Navy veteran and a Technical Lead Engineer at Boeing for the last 10 years. His debut book was inspired by the strength of his grandmother. He hopes their story will serve as inspiration for his three daughters and for readers everywhere. A longtime hobbyist photographer and currently a student at the University of Alabama, Aaron lives with his wife, Rachel, and is a proud father of three daughters, Kathleen, Ava, and Everly, and grandfather to Scarlet.

This Page Intentionally Left Blank

Preface

Like all stories, this little girl's story began shortly after she was born; when she was placed into a foster home. She would eventually become a civilian prisoner of war, and eventually in her own home.

"Rules of war" were supposed to protect her. She said they had no idea the things she would face in the years to come. She never dreamt of how a once beautiful place would become a place of horror and starvation.

Even though she survived a war where she was directly in the thick of it, for many years, she endured even more unspeakable horrors at the hands of a loved one, in the form of domestic abuse.

Her survival became the foundation of everything I am today, from her faith and strength, to her love and kindness, even her blunt honesty. Growing up, I would hear stories of her survival, stories that my mom told me, and stories I would hear directly from her. She was just one victim in the larger issue of domestic abuse. According to a source, UN Women, statistics in 2025, an estimated 840 million women, or 1 in 3 women, are subjected to some form of physical and/or sexual violence in their lifetime. That source goes on to say that globally, every day, an average of 137 women and girls die at the hands of an intimate partner or supposed loved one.

I am aware and want to acknowledge that every situation is different; socio-economic factors, the inability to distance themselves because of emotional and physical isolation, and countless other variables that prevent escaping the abuse and being killed. But she survived. She survived war, and she survived her abuser's torment, until it caught up to her. It was her instinct to survive, and for that reason, it's why my family's legacy even exists today. Her inspiration is responsible for my marriage, my three daughters, and my granddaughter. She taught me to never give up, to be strong, and to continue to try to be a better person. She wasn't trying to be an example; it was the way she lived her life. I knew that I could take what life threw at me and remain unbroken. She was Shirley Mae, and she was my Grandma.

Chapter 1

Echoes of Los Banos (The War Years)

Grandma's story would eventually finish with her fairytale ending, one she would pursue for decades. She would go on to eventually find her true happiness and love, marrying the love of her life, Lavar Bryson, until death did they part. Grandma's loved ones - Lavar, two of her children, my mom, and my Uncle Jimmy; surrounded her during her final moments. Grandma passed away on April 3, 2009. Her life ended on what she considered a good note; unfortunately, a life that began in war and the cumulative toll of abuse endured for so many years would have an irreversible effect.

Her life didn't begin as one would hope for or imagine. Shirley Mae was all alone, born on September 8th, 1939, in Washington, D.C., a year that marked the start of the Second World War between the Axis and the Allies. Her parents, Mattie Bernice Crawford and Edward E. Wissman, had given her up when she was born. Mattie was just 15 years old when Shirley Mae was born. At such a young age, she couldn't take the responsibility of a child and, consequently, gave Shirley up for adoption.

When she first opened her eyes, she did not feel the

warmth of a home or the embrace of a mother, but rather the chaos of an adoption home; a place where she was one of the many children waiting to get adopted. News of war had started spreading, and people had begun worrying about themselves and their children, but who would worry about poor little Shirley Mae? She had no one; no parents, no relatives, and no one who would care about her or whether she lived or died. This would change very soon for her, though.

Shortly after Shirley Mae was born, between 1940 and 1941, two US missionaries stationed in the Philippines, James A. Leland and Rosamond C. Leland would visit the orphanage she was in. The Lelands didn't have any biological children and arrived with the intentions of adopting a little boy. Instead, Shirley Mae caught their eye, and they decided to adopt her. After completing the paperwork, they brought Shirley Mae back to the Philippines with them. The Lelands instantly became her parents, two people who would finally love her the way she deserved. James was the first manager of the Philippine Publishing House from 1935 until 1941. He then served as the factory supervisor from 1941 to 1951. He was a reputable man, and people in town knew of him. When they adopted Shirley Mae, it became clear that she was in good hands and that the poor little orphan girl finally had a home at last.

In the chaos that was war, the United States was mostly in a supporting role for the Allied Forces. On December 7th, 1941, the Japanese attacked Pearl Harbor. Although this attack came as a surprise, Japan and the United States had been edging toward war for quite some time. In the devastating attack, the Japanese destroyed around 20 American ships and more than 300 airplanes were destroyed or damaged. More than 2000 people also lost their lives. It was then that Congress declared war on Japan, officially bringing America into World War II. Just hours later, on December 8th, the Japanese began invading the Philippines, bombing Clark Field, a prominent American air base on the Island of Luzon. It was clear in a matter of hours that the situation was dire.

Even though it was vulnerable, the Philippines was a strategic military location, which made it a key objective for both the Allies and the Axis. The American forces present in the Philippines were deemed helpless as the Japanese bombs rained on Clark Field. The sounds of explosions echoed throughout the island; jet engines of the Japanese aircraft were deafening as they made passes across the island. The normally vibrant sounds of the jungles, the birds chirping, all of which were now drowned out by the sounds of war. As the initial attacks came to a close, everything was silent except for the ringing in ears and people hearing the sound of their own breathing.

Everyone was scared and in shock, caught off guard. This also meant that the Lelands and Grandma were now behind enemy lines. With the smell of jet fumes from the aircraft and the wild, visible destruction from the bombs, people were afraid and anxious about what would happen next. Children were confused, seeing a fear on their parents' faces, along with everyone else around them.

Japanese authorities turned Los Baños into a holding area where over 1,500 Americans and other civilians were held captive. When Shirley Mae and her parents were taken to Los Banos, all they had were their clothes and a small wooden box with important, small items such as birth certificates. It had their last name, *Leland*, etched onto the top.

With everything going on, Shirley Mae did not know what to think, she had never seen so many people together in her life. The camp smelled awful, the stench of so many people who were unable to shower and change clothes like they used to before the invasion. Shirley Mae was surprised by how different all these people were. Some looked like her; others looked like her parents. Shirley Mae was only two when the Japanese invaded the Philippines. Being so young, she felt especially vulnerable to what was going on around her. She sometimes woke up to the sound of her own heartbeat and the deafening sirens around the island. She personally witnessed the trauma of people starving and getting sick daily. It was a lot for everyone, but for a two-year-old, it was next level. Violence, stress, severe anxiety, and physical and mental trauma became the norm in her life, which unfortunately, followed her throughout the rest of her life.

Initially, time in the camps wasn't as bad as everyone expected it to be; however, over time, the situation started deteriorating. Food became scarcer as the guards reduced what was available, and brutality became increasingly common. The food they did get was already stinking because it was starting to spoil by the time the guards allowed them to have any. Captives became so used to the fear that they almost lost hope of ever escaping the camps. Grandma and her parents would hide under the dinner table when the sirens would go off during air raids. She had just turned three and had been seeing war since what seemed like forever. She no longer smiled, it was as if she was almost too scared all the time, and now, being brought into a completely new life frightened her. She wanted to cling to her parents, not letting them go out of sight. She thought if she held them too tight, she could maybe save them.

She knew she was in the middle of a war, but despite that, she found her way to cope. Most days, Shirley Mae wouldn't have much to eat or anything else to keep her busy. She could see that the adults around her were constantly subjected to deprivation, hate, and violence, and she began to wonder if this was how her life was going to be from then on. She hadn't seen a world much different from the day she was born. As the Filipinos began an underground resistance, Japanese brutality grew. The war shone with all its hateful color, there was the withholding of food and medical supplies, local women were kidnapped and turned into sex laborers, facing threats of rape, kidnapping, torture, and even murder. And yet, the Filipinos showed grit. Women, who were the most vulnerable during the Japanese occupation, risked their lives to support the resistance by the guerrillas, not knowing the brutalities that awaited them.

The Los Baños camp had other children, too, some of the local citizens and others of American soldiers. When Shirley Mae saw other kids her age, she wanted to play. To her, this was her first experience of friendship; before the war, she was too young to have any friends. During a time of war in a prisoner camp, nothing about these new friendships was normal. Children played to distract themselves until a sudden blast, or a guard's grumble terrified them. On top of that, Shirley Mae constantly faced the trauma of being separated from her parents. The fear that she would once again be orphaned haunted her day and night, and in times like these, she would stay close to the Lelands, for if something happened to them, she wouldn't want to be apart.

Years had gone by; the Japanese were losing the war, and rumors were spreading that the Japanese were going to kill everyone they were holding captive. U.S. Intelligence increased surveillance to see if the rumors were true. The Japanese had dug trenches, stealing a page out of the Nazis' playbook, where they would lower the people and then shoot all of them into the trenches. There was panic. People started worrying about their lives more than ever. They desperately awaited a rescue but didn't know when or how it would happen. There were 250 Japanese guards constantly surveilling the fenced area. Rescuing more than 2000 people from a place like that needed planning because any mistake would mean casualties, thousands of them. The war didn't need any more casualties, especially not because of a lack of planning. There was simply no room for errors.

And then the day came. It was like any other day for Shirley Mae and her family in the camp when the most perfect rescue mission in modern history was being planned using the intel collected.

Led by Major Vanderpool, the 11th Airborne Division, now famously known among historians as *The Angels*, would begin training and preparing for a rescue at Los Banos. General MacArthur was quoted as saying, "Do what will best further the Allied cause," which essentially gave the 11th Airborne carte blanche. Operations began weeks prior, where Allied forces witnessed the horrors that the Japanese had inflicted elsewhere on the island. This made Los Banos such a high priority that General MacArthur personally showed up, giving the order to prepare for the liberation of Los Banos.

On the 23rd of February, 1945, early in the morning, around 7 am, as the Japanese guards looked up at the sky, all they could see were kite gliders being towed behind C-47s. The sky filled with white parachutes like flower blossoms falling from trees, as the paratroopers dropped in. The sight was no less than a horror for them. Inside, Shirley Mae held tight to her parents, just like the other kids in the camp. No one knew what was happening, but they could sense the chaos. And then, the shooting started. Most Japanese guards ended up getting shot by the troopers, but some managed to escape. However, they, were met by guerrillas waiting for them in the jungle with knives and machetes. The combined force of the guerrillas and the US soldiers took the Japanese by surprise, and before anyone realized what had happened, the prisoners were saved.

It was a confusing sight for Shirley Mae. Suddenly, seeing all these new people landing from the sky scared her, but then she saw the people around her; all cheering. Smiles were a rarity, but she knew whatever was happening, whoever these people were, they were here to help them. History would later call it one of the most successful rescue missions not only of the war, but in military history. That success was overshadowed though. To the world, the events on Iwo Jima, when the Marines hoisted up the flag, made what happened in Los Baños all but fade away, even though thousands were rescued.

She was almost six, but she was already aged beyond her years. She was a child of war and a survivor; something she would always continue being long after the rescue.

The Lelands continued to live in the Philippines as James worked as the factory supervisor of the Publishing House. The Philippine economy also began to improve, and as time passed, Shirley Mae was growing into a bright young girl who, although still carrying her trauma, the future appeared brighter than ever. And then, one day, July 26, 1951, while in his office, James clutched his chest as he was sitting at his desk having his cup of coffee...knocking over the cup, the coffee spilling, the news to follow, changed everything for Shirley Mae. James, Shirley Mae's dear father, had passed away due to a heart attack when she was only 11. Evidently, the war and living in the prisoner camp had taken a toll on his health, and his body couldn't take it anymore. After James' death, Rosamond took Shirley Mae back to the United States.

Rosamond would eventually remarry stateside with Shirley Mae still living with her. She was never the same after James' death, and the sight of Shirley Mae only stirred up memories and pain, pain that Rosamond was not willing to live with.

One morning, the sound of a suitcase zipper broke the silence in their home. A suitcase filled with everything Shirley Mae had owned stood next to her, she was in denial and shock. Shirley Mae counted every breathe, every step she took as she was escorted towards the front door, for what seemed like an eternity. Shirley Mae watched as her suitcase was placed in the back of the car, the trunk slammed shut. Shirley Mae was leaving for good, Rosamond placed Shirley Mae back in the foster system. She watched out the back window of the car as it took her away from her home, tears running down her cheeks. As everything would fade in the distance, she noticed the kids next door outside playing games, the last time she would ever see them. Shirley Mae was only 13, and abandoned yet again, what she feared the most - she was once again on her own in a cold-hearted world.

Chapter 2
Searching for Safety

Several years went by with Shirley Mae in the foster system, when God was merciful to her. She met James Windham in San Diego during the late 1950s. James was in the Navy; he was strong, smart, and everything that a young girl wanted in her life partner. Before she knew it, Shirley Mae was in love.

She felt for him what she had not felt for anyone ever. He stirred feelings up in her, made her feel safe, something she had struggled with her entire life. Soon after, Shirley Mae and James conceived my mom, Sherry Mae. The two were over the moon and finally a family. After a couple of years, Shirley Mae conceived again, and this time, it was a boy, James, my Uncle Jimmy. They were complete now, a stereotypical American family.

Shirley Mae had finally made a home, her place in the world. After everything she had gone through in her short time on this Earth, she thought this was it; this was where she would finally get comfortable and live a life with her children and husband like every other woman she knew.

My mom, Sherry, with my granddaughter, Scarlet.

However, life had different plans for her. This chapter, both in this book, and in her own life; was coming to a close. Soon, things between her and James began deteriorating. The love that once brought them together faded, and now they were stuck together in a meaningless relationship that both of them continued because they had to, not because they wanted to. They didn't want their children to go through the trauma of having divorced parents, but deep inside, they knew that they couldn't possibly live a lie. They were both young and had their entire lives ahead of them. They knew it wouldn't be fair to the kids, as kids always know something isn't right. And so, Shirley Mae and James decided to part ways. Shirley Mae was obviously devastated. She felt as if the world had abandoned her once again, left her on her own. But this time, she was not alone; she had her children with her.

After parting ways with James, Shirley Mae least expected to meet anyone; at least, she wasn't actively looking for a relationship and wanted to spend all her time with her kids. They had moved to Las Vegas looking for a new life. That's when fate brought Jack Delbert Sills into her life. A very charismatic man, Jack was 25 years old at the time and made his living in the roofing business when he met Shirley Mae. Jack was born in 1933 in Henryetta, Oklahoma. He said everything she wanted to hear, and most importantly to her, Shirley Mae's previous marriage and two children did not bother him. For Shirley, this was especially comforting; she thought that life had given her a second chance at love, so she grabbed the opportunity with both hands and married Jack on December 12, 1959.

Chapter 3
The Household of Hell

The initial years of her marriage were nothing out of the ordinary. Like any other couple, Shirley Mae and Jack lived a typical life where he went to work, and she stayed at home taking care of the house and the children. Shirley Mae also gave birth to a baby girl whom they named Shelly. Eventually, they would relocate to Boise, Idaho. Life was not easy, but it wasn't too bad either, when Jack was sober. However, with time, Shirley Mae began seeing Jack's true colors. She started noticing how Jack would humiliate her, get extremely angry occasionally, and not care about how his words made her feel. Jack was mostly drunk all the time and did not care about anyone, not even her.

Every time they would be with friends and family, he wouldn't think twice before being abusive, sometimes physically, sometimes verbally. He would insult her and say the most demeaning things about her past that would completely shatter her self-esteem and confidence. In those moments, Shirley Mae felt like digging a hole in the ground and crawling inside to avoid the stares and judgement.

There was nothing she felt that she could do. She was too young to be divorced for a second time. And now she had three children to worry about if she had left Jack, a seemingly daunting task for Shirley Mae. She had to survive despite how complicated everything was. Her life was now filled with fear and helplessness. The man of her house often threatened her to the point where she started fearing for her life and the lives of her children.

There were incidents when Jack's rage would take over, and she would have to call the police. Sometimes an officer would stay at the house with Jack until he cooled off and he could not follow, while another officer took Shirley and the kids to a motel in Boise. Eventually, on September 13, 1973, Jack had threatened Shirley and her children with a gun. Shirley had been living separately from Jack at the time and was living in Caldwell, Idaho. Jack used the gun to force her away and go back to his home. Jack was arrested and arraigned on Friday the 14th, but that didn't mean anything to Jack; it wouldn't stop the abuse. If anything, it probably pushed him further. Involving another woman after Shirley Mae, there was another arrest in May of 1982 when Jack was charged with felony battery with the intent to commit rape. This was another of the many times that Jack showed how evil he was.

Perhaps there were always signs. Jack had always been a cold man. He was unforgiving and would do anything to get back at someone who had even slightly hurt his ego. His ruthless personality sometimes shone from inside, and it was almost impossible to look past it.

Jack and Shirley would eventually move to Las Vegas,

Nevada, where Jack was a part of a union for his work. After moving there, Jack had mentioned a man named Fred and said something was going to happen to him. He would keep mentioning Fred and making it sound like he had stolen from him. Shirley Mae would barely answer because she knew exactly how dangerous it could be if he didn't like what she said. Jack and Fred worked together in the same union.

It had been going on for a while, and one day, the family had to go out. Jack was driving, and even though he wasn't always a rash driver, that day, he drove as if his life depended on it. He ran past the stop signal, and that's when he saw Fred, the guy he had been rambling about for days, crossing the street. It was like Jack knew he was going to be there. Jack ran over him without a second thought, shocking everyone in the car. Even though it was all his fault, Jack did not turn around and acknowledge the badly injured man lying on the road. He left him bleeding on the road as if nothing had happened. Shirley Mae couldn't help but feel both sad and frightened. Her husband had taken a man's life and did not show any remorse. She knew that something was wrong with him. She recalled that Jack had let it slip at one point how Fred had gone against the union in some way, and he was asked to kill Fred. Unfortunately for Shirley, Nevada had a law called Marital Privilege. Jack used this against Shirley; she was not allowed to legally testify against Jack in court if she tried to say anything to the police.

Shirley's words fell on deaf ears. Jack was always lost in

his rage, especially after that incident. The days that followed were filled with awkward silences. Whenever Shirley Mae thought of that day, she could hear the screeching tires that almost deafened her, followed by the sick thud. They had already hit the man before she could process what was happening. Her heart sank when Jack dismissively said that the man owed him money, even though already Jack mentioned it had something to do with the union. He must have forgotten, maybe not. Either way, the guilt settled over her, suffocating and consuming. She couldn't get that image out of her head. She wasn't sure what she had done to deserve the life that she was in.

Even though she had attempted to leave many times before, after that day, Shirley Mae knew she had to get away from Jack no matter what, a line had been crossed, even though it had technically been crossed years before. She didn't care about being divorced the second time or what people would think of her; she only cared about the well-being of her children. That was when she began plotting to run away from home. Jack wouldn't let her go that easily, and she knew that, so she had to go behind his back and run away to save her life and the lives of her children.

Jack was a heavy drinker, which Shirley Mae didn't like; however, she had decided to use it for her own benefit. Every night, she would wait for Jack to pass out, when she would begin planning her escape. She'd pack a bag, put everything she really needed, grab her kids, and tiptoe toward the back door, since it was not as loud as the front door. But, unfortunately, no matter how quiet she was, Jack always caught her. The first time he caught her, he was furious. He wasn't expecting her to run away, taking his daughter with him. He hit her, screamed at her at the top of his lungs regardless of how late it was at night, and then went to bed. That was the more mild of his reactions, other times he had been known to stomp on her back and neck and kick her while she was down, sometimes kicking her in the head. She would sustain injuries that shocked her doctors 30 years later, injuries that caused the doctors to think she had been in a car accident. She was never in a car accident.

The experience traumatized Shirley Mae, but it was never her last try. After a few days, she tried again. To her surprise, Jack caught her again. This time, he was angrier than before because he didn't think she would disobey him after what had happened the last time. Again, he hit her, shouted like a madman, and then went to bed, leaving Shirley Mae and the kids petrified.

It became a weekly thing; Shirley Mae would try running away and would get caught, but with every attempt, Jack's anger subsided. Perhaps he thought she'd never be able to get away, and he shouldn't waste his energy on her. What he didn't realize was that Shirley Mae wasn't going to give up that easily. She had decided to leave the life of fear and helplessness behind her and start fresh. For the first time in a very long time, she was hopeful that a better future awaited her and her children. And so, the day came when Shirley's attempt to escape finally succeeded. It was just like any other night; Jack was passed out with a bottle of liquor in his hand. When Shirley Mae realized he was out cold, she took out her bag from the cupboard with all her and her children's clothes and necessary belongings and began heading toward the door. She tiptoed toward it and then closed the door silently behind her. Jack hadn't come running after her yet; that was certainly a good sign. She crept down the stairs, shushing the children so they wouldn't wake Jack, and before she knew it, she was out. Shirley Mae couldn't believe she had finally made it; she was actually free from the house of hell.

Shirley Mae was out in the world again, but she had never lived independently, caring for herself and her kids' needs. However, she was confident that whatever life she gave her children would be better than the one they had at Jack's. With her, they weren't terrified all the time. In fact, with her, they were the safest. She didn't have to be worried about their security as she lived in her own house, because no one was safe around Jack, not even the kids.

It was a big decision to run away from the house, but it wasn't made easily; it took time. Any more days Shirley Mae might've spent with Jack could have seriously ended worse for her and her children, and she was not going to risk it. But here she was now, all alone in a big, cold world that didn't favor women, especially at the time. She was scared. She had no proper accommodation and had to spend the first few months in a motel. As time passed, the reality started to settle in, and a fear of the unknown crept into her heart. Running away had been a desperate act, one that was primarily fueled by her instinct to protect her children, but now, when she was finally free, an unsettling loneliness surrounded her.

The truth is, because of her childhood, Shirley Mae always dreamt for someone to want and love her, providing a happy home. She knew she would find the strength for her children even if she didn't know she had it in her.

As a mother, Shirley Mae knew life wasn't going to be any easier, it was actually going to be harder before it got better, but despite that, she'd have to figure things out. When everyone was asleep, she would plan and visualize their life ahead.

As weeks began to turn into months, Shirley Mae picked herself up. She had learned to be alone and work through the challenges that came her way, but she still longed for someone that would love her and the kids. While she wasn't actively searching, life worked in her favor when she met Donald Cadotte, or Don. Don, born in Minnesota on June 9, 1927, was a complete gentleman. He was nothing like Jack or any other man Shirley Mae had met before. Shirley Mae immediately noticed his kind demeanor as he listened to her recount the traumatic experiences she faced through the years. Every word she spoke revealed the pain and struggles she had endured; all of those moments of fear and heartbreak that had left permanent scars on her soul.

As their friendship deepened, something beautiful began to unfold between them. His affection grew for her, and they would often find themselves drawn to one another, the bond they formed becoming a shelter for Shirley Mae. And before they knew it, they were in love. She could not believe she had finally found someone who genuinely loved and cared for her. This new chapter carried skepticism. She had searched for this kind of connection, but the memories of her past reminded her how elusive that was. She wasn't sure if she would be able to trust again or genuinely be able to allow anyone inside the walls she built up. There was always a constant fear of being hurt or abandoned again.

Despite all her doubts, it was the first time Shirley Mae smiled in a really long time. Don and Shirley would marry on November 28, 1973, in Elko, Nevada. With Don, she experienced a nurturing and respectful love, a stark contrast to the torment she had endured with her ex-husband, Jack. Don embraced not only her but also her three children with open arms. He worked to earn their trust, providing a home full of warmth, laughter, and that sense of belonging. Unfortunately for Shirley, the remnants of the trauma were always there. On the surface, everything seemed calm, but deep down, she coped with the echoes of her past, unsure if she would ever be entirely free of them.

Then, one night, something happened that worsened her

fears. She and Don were in bed like any other night when the sound of shattering glass jolted Shirley Mae awake. The piercing sound sent a chill down her spine. Her heart jumped from her chest as she impulsively reached for Don. She soon realized what was happening. Jack, her abusive ex-husband, was coming through their window, a gun in his hand – he had found Shirley Mae. She pointed toward the man in the window. Her face was white with fear, her life flashing in front of her eyes. The past, which had been haunting her for so long, was now in front of her, and she was frozen.

As soon as Don realized what was happening, he acted. He had vowed to keep Shirley Mae safe, and he planned to make good on that promise. In that instant, Shirley Mae's world felt fragile. Don tightened his hold around her, and without any hesitation, he reached for the gun in his nightstand. And with that, Don fired at Jack. The shot rang out, and Jack stumbled back, wounded but still alive. He fled into the darkness, leaving behind a shattered window and a sense of chaos that disrupted peace. In the immediate aftermath, relief flooded Shirley Mae, though bitterness also marked the moment. Jack had been a haunting figure from her past, a reminder of the violence and fear she had fought so hard to escape.

However, that night's aftermath brought a different kind of turmoil. The fear did not vanish; it lingered intrusively in her thoughts. Every creak or groan in the house, or slightest wind outside, kept her on edge. Yet through it all, Don remained by her side. He became her harbor in the storm, offering support and reassurance that she and her children weren't alone. When she had nightmares, he held her tightly, whispering words of comfort.

With Don by her side, Shirley Mae began to embrace the future. Eventually, she let go of her fears when she heard Jack had escaped back to Oklahoma. Slowly, the flicker of hope she had felt in the aftermath of that night began to grow. As Shirley Mae and Don navigated the challenges together, she embraced the possibility of joy once more. She clung to the hope that he would never return to their lives, and now that he was gone for good, she could rebuild her life. Each day, she grew a little braver, a little more determined to create a life filled with love, laughter, and security. And as spring blossomed into summer, she knew that no matter what challenges lay ahead, she and Don would face them together, united in their journey toward healing and happiness. She had finally understood that true love was about unwavering support, mutual respect, and the courage to face life together.

Shirley and Don were not destined to be together forever, as they would eventually divorce years later. It wasn't because he was an evil man who didn't love her. Quite the opposite, she had finally found someone who truly loved her. That chapter of her life laid the foundation that taught Shirley that she was good enough to be loved and would finally be able to love and trust someone again. That someone would eventually be Lavar Bryson. Lavar would be her ultimate success in finding her soulmate.

Lavar would do anything for my grandma. His heart was kind and welcoming. He saw my mom as one of his own children and my brother and me as his own grandkids. He was a cowboy at heart who used to rodeo until he got injured. Even after his injuries, he continued to ride horses and even gave my mom her first horse, Princess. My mom had always loved horses, but we were never in the position to be able to afford or own one. My grandma and mom were the happiest they had been now that grandma had finally found true happiness. Just before we moved back and a few days after my 16th birthday, Grandma and Lavar would finally get married on April 15, 1992, at the Elko County Courthouse.

I never personally witnessed my grandma face all the battles she did, but I definitely heard about them growing up from grandma herself and my mom.

Chapter 4
Heirlooms and Legacy

When I was younger, my mom would tell me about the amazing woman my grandma was and how she had endured all the problems throughout her life, yet she still raised her children to be responsible adults. Listening to the stories would always give me goosebumps, I was humbled and honored to be related to a woman like Shirley Mae.

I can't help but look back on the times I spent with Grandma, whose quiet strength left a permanent mark on my life. I still remember sitting with Grandma when we lived across the street from my Aunt Polly and my cousins. We would sit there listening to the stories while she held her coffee and her skinny brown cigarettes. Reflecting on a journey that was filled with adversity, violence, and unwavering positivity; I realize how her struggles shaped not only my mom but, ultimately, myself. In her stories, I found lessons of courage and hope that became the foundation on which I built my understanding of life, even if those lessons were not always clear and apparent at the time. Growing up, either my grandma lived with us or we lived with her, especially during our transition to Nevada. There were just a few short times when we didn't live together.

Those years were rich with laughter, warmth, and a sense

of security despite the struggles we faced as a family. The walls of our home echoed with her stories, each one a proof of her ability to persist. I would sit cross-legged on the living room floor, hanging on her every word, absorbing her experiences like a sponge. She would often have me sit in front of her as she began one of her stories. Through her stories, I learned more about her life, marked by the constant violence that shadowed her life.

Yet, somehow, she always managed to emerge stronger. "I witnessed things that would make most people crumble," she would say, "But I found God and refused to be a victim." I could see it in her eyes, but I could also see the years of fight she had put in and the hurt she had endured doing that. I recently found an article from the October 28, 1976, issue of the Idaho Statesman, when I was roughly six months old. A journalist named Tim Woodward interviewed Grandma, who was 37 at that time. Woodward captured a recurring bad dream that haunted her. She is waiting at an airport when a plane lands, and a woman disembarks and approaches Shirley. Woodward wrote, in the dreams, as Shirley and the woman speak with each other, she realizes the woman is not identifiable, faceless. The woman who has no face is the mother she never met. Outside of being born, this was her only interaction with her mother up to this point in her life. Her mother, Mattie Bernice Crawford, lived in the Florence Crittenton Home for unwed mothers in D.C. when Grandma was born.

My Grandma considered her childhood a happy one, according to the article, even though she spent much of it in the Japanese internment camp. Even after living in the foster system from when she was 13 until she was 18, she had never stopped thinking about her mother. She had been looking for her without any luck. Grandma was 37 years old when she was interviewed for the article, so she had actively been looking for 19 years. But she still somehow hung on to hope; she just knew that her mother was looking for too. Grandma would eventually find her mother several years later.

Despite how many troubles she had seen in her life, Grandma always stayed positive and looked for solutions rather than seeing just the problems. This remarkable ability to remain positive was a guiding light for us all. When she talked about moving from place to place, always seeking safety, be it after her marriage to Jack or when she was a little girl and had to move places in order to be safe during the war, I could feel her struggles but also the lightness of her spirit. She knew that one could easily become another statistic, but wallowing in self-pity was not the solution she would settle for. Instead, every day was a new chance to improve her situation for herself and her children, no matter how tough things got.

I learned early on in my life that socio-economic circumstances could affect a person's trajectory, but they didn't have to define it. We were never homeless, yet our lives drifted at the poverty line. I witnessed the toll it took on my mom, who worked multiple jobs to keep us afloat. The positive thing was that Grandma's strength was always there to lead us, becoming a beacon of hope in our lives, guiding my mother to raise me with that same spirit. She would tell my mom that we can't let the system weigh us down; instead, we have to use it as motivation to rise higher above all the hurdles and problems that come our way.

One of the most critical life lessons I learned was that life was not kind and would continuously throw curveballs at you. Not everyone can overcome obstacles thrown their way, and I was taught to never judge anyone because of their situation. It isn't anyone's fault if they tried, and if they never try, even then, we never judge. That was always the message I took from watching not just grandma, or mom, but people like my dad, and my aunts and uncles on both sides of my family. I saw the nice things you can have by working hard. It was okay to stumble as long as we dared to step back up to the plate and keep swinging at our goals. We need to understand that there are no strikeouts in life. Yes, you would fail, but your failures are not the end of the world; in fact, they are just another mechanism to learn and improve. So, rather than shying away from mistakes, one should embrace them.

There have been many challenging times in my life, both as a child and as a grown-up, but each time, the lessons I learned from Grandma proved to be life-changing. Every time I would feel down, Grandma's presence was something I could lean on. She had a distinct warmth about her that one could feel in her presence, even when she had not said a word to you.

It was reassuring knowing that there was someone who would constantly support me and tell me that it was just one fall: Get up, dust yourself off, and try again. In the end, what matters is how you respond to setbacks.

I could let failures define me, or I could learn from them and push forward. It's kind of funny because, in a way, those failures still do define you, whether you learn or not. Taking her advice to heart, I always worked extremely hard in whatever I did and never let small bumps and hurdles stop me from achieving my goals. Life would be far from perfect, though, and there were times I lost my way, letting my grandma's wisdom briefly slip away, making all the wrong decisions. I definitely had some failures along the way.

Grandma's influence extended beyond her stories; it filled the very fabric of our daily lives. She instilled in us the belief that every moment held the potential for positivity. I remember mornings and nights filled with her laughter. Her positivity was so contagious that it made the rest of us happy. She started all her days with gratitude, reminding us that no matter what's coming our way, there's always something to be thankful for.

Even though these might seem like small lessons, they played a significant part in our daily routines and formed the backbone of my understanding of resilience. This is why, even in struggle, we found ways to celebrate our blessings through our successes and failures. I learned to view challenges as opportunities for growth, and this perspective became my compass, guiding my path even as I transitioned into adulthood.

As I grew older and Grandma left us, we looked for her in her stories and in the heirlooms she left us. Even though nothing could match her presence, these things became a reminder that she was once among us and that she was perhaps the most amazing woman I have ever met.

My mom has a trunk that Grandma passed down to her, with lots of old photos, letters, spent ammunition shells, and a bunch of other stuff, and I remember looking inside it and exploring its contents often. I still remember having the occasional show and tell in grade school, and I would bring some of those contents to school and share stories with my classmates. To this day, that trunk reminds us all of her memories, telling stories and sharing her wisdom. My aunt Shelly has another trunk with some old memories left behind from Grandma's life. I also have a dinner table in my house and a small trunk that was carried into the Japanese Internment camp at the time of the war.

When I moved through life, the lessons she conveyed became more than just wisdom; they became a part of my identity. I found myself in situations where I stood up against the wrong, no matter how hard it was. I discovered a passion for justice, driven by the belief that everyone, including myself, deserves a chance to thrive, regardless of their circumstances.

As I continue to navigate the complexities of life, I carry her lessons with me like armor. I remind myself daily of the strength that runs through my family; a legacy built on strength and love. I strive to live a life filled with gratitude, positivity, and unwavering determination.

Each time I face a challenge, I do so with the belief that there are opportunities for growth and transformation; I can learn from my mistakes and keep moving forward. If she were here with me today, I would tell her how much she and every word she has ever spoken affected my life and made me the person I am today. I would thank her for being soft and nurturing despite having a difficult life. I would thank her for sharing her vulnerable moments with me and for trusting me to learn from them. And most importantly, I would tell her how much I love her.

Trunk that my Grandmother's parents had made in Philippines, sitting at Mom's house today.

Chapter 5
My Beginnings

I was born on April 11, 1976, a bicentennial baby, and my little brother, Roy, followed on September 21, 1978. We were close; inseparable, really; and fiercely protective of one another. We had each other's backs through everything, even though there were times we couldn't stand to even hear each other breathe, or make other annoying sounds like crunching on chips. We were always fighting, sometimes big enough fights to knock over furniture. Even then, our bond was built on loyalty and a kind of unspoken understanding: I could mess with him, but no one else could. That kind of closeness was rare, and I never took it for granted.

My brother and I when we were little. Not sure how old we were.

Thinking back to my childhood, I recall that I was very moral. I was a very modest, skinny kid growing up, but much stronger for my size than most would realize. I was scrappy. I never threw punches or kicks because I fought with the intent to deescalate, restrain, not hurt anyone. Whenever someone was being bullied or picked on, and I witnessed it, I would feel the need to stand up for them. Sure, there were times I made myself a target with the other person, but it was never just about myself, and I had no problems taking care of myself.

I stood up to them, not because I wanted to fight, but because I couldn't stand by and see someone who couldn't or wouldn't stand up for themselves, and sometimes this was Roy.

He could have a big mouth and talk trash, sometimes not able to back it up. I still remember this one scrap with John, a tall and lanky kid from just outside of our neighborhood. I will admit that it was my brother's own damn fault for throwing a rock at John first, even though John had on a bike helmet. It was kind of funny. John had been provoking my brother all afternoon, and Roy finally had enough. Roy shouldn't have thrown the rock, but that did not mean I was going to let John pound on him because of that. So, obviously, being the big brother, I had to step in and protect my little brother, something that I would eventually fail at.

John was a little socially awkward and didn't have many friends. I used to enjoy hanging out with him and riding our bikes around our little hometown in Florala, Alabama, but that didn't mean he could do what he wanted around me. I still remember the front of house barely being visible because of the giant azalea bushes out front.

John was bigger than both Roy and me, and a little bit older, I think. He was homeschooled I think, so I don't remember even seeing him at school. When John went after my brother, I jumped on him, taking him to the ground just as he was about to punch Roy. I did what I normally would do, and I put him in a chokehold and made myself heavy so he couldn't get back up. Everyone always knew Roy and I had each other's backs. After the scuffle, we would go on to play with John another day, no hard feelings or grudges.

Growing up, like most kids, I attended public schools, starting with Florala City School and moving around as life required, two elementary schools early on, between kindergarten and eighth grade. The other school was in Forest, Mississippi, for second grade. Although I did pay attention in all of my classes, it was science and history that always fascinated me the most, and eventually, art. Art was something I never knew I had in me, but would become my main outlet with all the eventual moving around. When I was drawing, I could lose myself for hours on end.

In those early school years, I grew up with a solid group of friends. Some of us even joined the Boy Scouts together. My mom was our Den Leader, which brought a sense of unity to our little troop. Almost everyone in town knew my mom since she also worked at the newspaper, and our family was also well-known, with an uncle that was a local police officer. That didn't matter, though, when the Scouts decided to bar female leaders. None of the local men stepped up, so that part of our lives quietly ended. Still, I kept the same group of friends from kindergarten through eighth grade. You could always find some of us riding our bikes around town or having a sleepover at someone's house for a birthday, or just because. We would even venture over to a town called Crestview, Florida, for my birthdays, where there was a movie theater and a Pizza Hut.

Not all the kids I called friends were good for me. I also tended to gravitate toward kids who had problems at home, kids whom others avoided. One of them was a kid named Philip Carr. He was older than the rest of us, having been held back a time or two. He wasn't the sharpest kid, but we played together often since he lived down the street, just a few blocks away. To me, he was just another kid trying to find his place, something I could relate to. If memory serves me correctly, I think Philip was in the Boy Scouts for a little while as well. There was one time I remember getting in trouble because I traded my new calculator watch to him for just a regular Casio. I knew it was harder for his parents to be able to get him something like that, so I just wanted to help the way a 10-year-old would. Then, out of nowhere, everything changed.

When he was twelve, Philip shocked our little town when he repeatedly stabbed and killed his mother over a fight about dinner. My mom, who worked as both a journalist and a magistrate, was involved with the case and told me what happened. I was stunned. A boy who had been in our home, whom I had called a friend, had done something unthinkable. That was the moment I realized how little we sometimes know the people around us, but I still had that core group of friends that I knew were good people. That would all change one day after my parents would split up. It was soon after, that we were moving every year for the next four years; it became harder to hold onto people.

Senior photo from high school.

All of a sudden, I was the new guy everywhere, I started feeling like the person nobody knew, mainly because I actually was.

Even though I thought of myself as an outgoing person in my early childhood, being that new guy, I was not as outgoing as I thought. It was when I moved to another school that I realized how shy I was and not, in fact, the social magnet I thought I was. Having the same friends all through my early childhood gave me that false sense.

We had to move halfway through 8th grade, and even though I was a bit forlorn that I had to leave my friends, I was looking forward to making new ones at a new school. However, I soon came to understand that my shy and quiet demeanor would actually be the dominant side of my personality, and the main reason I had grown close to my friends from my previous life was that we had known each other since grade school. It was really a struggle for me to adjust to a new environment, but eventually, I found my place with a new group of friends in a new town.

Every time I changed schools, the teachers took a liking to me because of my studious nature and serious attitude. Even though I had friends my age, I was always comfortable and connected to the adults in my life. I was always an upbeat, smart student, and even through my shy nature, I made sure to participate in school events because they challenged me, especially the spelling bees in grade school. I always enjoyed taking part in the spelling bee in my earlier school years, usually performing very well. I wasn't perfect, but paired with my disciplined nature and willingness to learn made me an easy student for my teachers to like.

I was and still have many faults to this day, with probably

the biggest one being the ability to cruise through school with little effort, not giving my 100%. I did work very hard and focused, but I always held back because I could. I was always on the honor roll for grades, even had perfect attendance for most of my school career. When I participated in those spelling bee competitions and performed very well, deep down, I knew that if I had given more effort, I surely would have done even better. Not ridding myself of this habit has always been one of my biggest shortcomings. Still, I made sure to always focus and put forth the efforts to further my knowledge, but I was and always am a kid at heart, even if I always looked serious on the outside.

As a kid, I used to love playing alone in my room with my He-Man, G.I. Joe, and Transformers figures. It used to drive Roy crazy that I could play alone for hours since he always had to be around someone. He was the social one in our family. When outside, we used to love "getting lost" in the woods. Roy and I were always outdoor kids, and the dense wooded areas with swamps and the life that was teeming in the woods always piqued my curiosity. It was a punishment if anything other than the weather relegated us to playing inside. If we weren't in the woods, we found ourselves playing sports as well: baseball, basketball, and football. Everyone would come to our yard to play because we had a big double lot clear for us to play all the things. I was always the fastest kid in a foot race growing up, so I loved playing anything that showcased my speed. So much so, I was told by a coach at my second high school that I should play football, but I was scared that if I got caught, the kids who were twice my size would crush me. I did try out for cross country, but I never got to participate because of an issue with my birth certificate not being the correct version.

When I was not out in the woods exploring or playing sports, you could find me inside watching TV with my parents, who had a rather complicated relationship. There was always a quiet tenseness. From the outside, they seemed to have a strong relationship. At first, they were solid. My dad, raised in the Mormon Church, had walked away from his faith when he married my mom, but his upbringing lingered in how he saw the world. He was firm but never cruel. If Roy and I argued too much - which happened often - we would get the belt, a switch, or a small tap in the back of the head, occasionally a little tug on the hair behind our ears. It was mostly Roy that got it, he was always in trouble for something, mostly because he wasn't smart about being dumb. We didn't feel like our punishments were abusive or anything; it was a different day and age back then compared to today. It was never about punishment as much as it was about setting boundaries and knowing them. My mom didn't see it that way, though, and over time, that became a serious point of contention between them.

My parents divorced around the time I was thirteen, but in truth, the signs had been there for a while. Dad worked offshore on the oil rigs; two weeks out, two weeks home; and when he was home, he picked up work as a roofer or carpenter. They loved each other; there was no doubt. He knew my mom was pregnant with me before they got married, and he didn't flinch. I think carrying that secret took a toll on them. Maybe it was that, or maybe it was the growing differences in how they viewed life and parenting.

Even as a kid, I could sense the growing tension between them, a quiet drift that widened with each passing year. My mom was yearning for her own sense of independence, wanting to work, to contribute, to be something more than just a homemaker. My dad, on the other hand, came from a more old-fashioned way of thinking; he believed a woman's place was in the home, and he didn't see the need for her to take on a job outside the house. He was almost always away on the oil rigs, gone for long stretches of time, which only added to the strain. Their paths and priorities had started pulling in different directions, and eventually, the space between them became too wide to ignore.

I'm sure there were other reasons as well, but the bottom line is that the marriage didn't last. Funny enough, even now, Dad still talks about her as "the one that got away." Bring her up in conversation, and there's always a pause, a softness in his voice. Even though she holds a place in his heart to this day, he is so very happy with my current step-mom, Angelica. She has been the best thing in his life for the longest time.

When they divorced, I didn't see it coming. Sure, they fought, but that seemed normal to me. I thought everyone's parents fought. I had no idea their relationship was truly breaking down. I was barely 13 when it finally happened. It hit Roy and me hard. I tried to stay strong, to be the one holding it all together, but Roy took it especially hard. When we would go from one house to the other between parents, he'd cry. I cried too, but always on the inside. I never liked revealing my tears because I wanted to look strong.

Mom and Dad both moved on pretty quick. Dad had met Susan, Mom had met Curt. Curt had a son, John that was closer to Roy's age which was awesome since we could all relate. Susan had two kids of her own, Becky and David. They were younger than Roy and I, but they were great and we all got along. Dad and Susan married pretty quickly, with the four of us kids being a part of the wedding. Mom and Curt dated for a while, but they would also go on to get married.

Initially, I chose to live with my mom, while Roy chose to live with my dad. I wanted to make sure our parents had one of us so they wouldn't be alone. I had this naive idea that I could split my time evenly and float between them like a pendulum. But that illusion broke quickly. One summer between eighth and ninth grade, I was supposed to return to my mom's, but on the night before I was going to fly back to Nevada, I called her. *"Mom, I'm not coming home this time. I'm going to stay with Dad,"* I told her, with shaking in my voice. I can still hear the break in her voice. I could hear her start to cry. What had I just done? She didn't have Roy, and now she didn't have me. That has stuck with me to this day. If Roy had been with her, I probably would've stayed with Dad; I just didn't want either of them to be alone. After ninth grade, my mom and Curt moved from Nevada back to Alabama in Andalusia. There was also John, Curt's son, whom I see as my brother to this day, so the move was to be closer to us kids. I moved back in with my mom and stayed with her and Curt during my 10th grade year. It wasn't the last time we would move, though. At the end of tenth grade, we moved back to Nevada.

We had nothing because of this move being so costly. Mom and Curt worked at a local cotton gin in Andalusia, where they didn't make much money at all. It was the reason we made the move back to Nevada, so Curt could work at the same gold mines he had worked at when we moved there in eighth grade. Mom and I would get on an Amtrak train to ride all the way from Mobile, Alabama, to Elko, Nevada. We had nothing when we got there, so we moved in with Grandma and her fourth and final husband, Lavar. Even though I had heard about bits and pieces of my Grandma's life through the years, it never resonated with me until I got a little older. It was living with her one last time that I finally heard more details, and I came to understand what type of woman she was.

Me getting ready to graduate high school in Elko, Nevada.

On the surface, she was just Grandma, a loving and consistent presence in my life who seemed like any other family member at first glance. However, as I grew older, I came to realize she was my symbol of strength from a very humble and difficult beginning.

My Grandma's story was one of unimaginable hardship and resilience. Her life was riddled with challenges that would have broken most people, but despite facing such enormous obstacles, she refused to be defined by those circumstances and trudged along. She isn't the first or last woman to face adversity, but to me, her story is unique and worth sharing. From the very day she was born, she was faced with not being wanted by her mother, to enduring the turmoil of a world at war and survival. Through it all, she maintained a spirit that inspired those around her and left a mark on future generations.

What should have been a time of innocence and joy became a harrowing struggle for survival. Yet, even in the face of such adversity, she found moments of light.

She had many defining moments in her life, ones that underscored her belief in the importance of perseverance and the will to survive. Periods of her life were marked by instability and uncertainty, yet she began to develop the inner strength that would come to define her. Her early childhood experiences shaped her worldview and instilled in her a deep sense of gratitude and determination. Despite the hardships she faced, Grandma never saw herself as a victim. Instead, she used her experiences as fuel to move forward, to adapt, and to build a better life for herself and her family. She often told me that the key to strength wasn't just enduring hard times but choosing to learn and grow from them.

Her lessons weren't just about survival; they were about finding purpose in the face of adversity. When life became difficult, she would remind those around her that it could always be worse, not as a way to diminish our struggles but to encourage us to find perspective and strength. Our family isn't the only one or the first that has gone through some serious shit, her story, and even my own story isn't meant to be "woe is me". Her story goes back to an exact moment in time where her end would have meant no beginning for her future family and me, and for countless others, because of all the connections we made. It's those ripples, the other lives that have been affected because of the life I have lived, the good and the bad parts.

Living with her at sixteen, hearing those details of Los Baños, her time in the foster system, and her time with Jack, all in her own voice, made those stories finally resonate with me as a symbol of strength rather than just family lore.

Chapter 6
The Foundation

I did not have the best childhood in terms of schooling, not due to problems with my academic performance or behavior, but as I mentioned before, it was the fact that I had to change schools six times. I saw three high schools alone, which is twice as many as an average high school teenager.

In most cases, such a rocky childhood would throw off anyone. The impacts from academic gaps because of the different requirements, loss of identity, and emotional stress are just some of the things resulting from the moving around. There are typically some positives associated with all that moving, though. I was more resilient, had enhanced social skills, even if I was quiet, I learned to be friends with a wide variety of people at an early age, and the main thing that I still benefit from to this day is my adaptability. Imagine changing schools 3 times in the span of 4 years. Not only changing schools, but also three states, and needing to adjust to them in such a short period of time. However, thankfully, I always had my studies in check. Not only that, but ever since middle school, I had always been one of those children who had an extra pencil or two, had their hand raised for many of the questions asked by the teacher, and submitted their homework on time.

Me in Army JROTC in 10th grade in Andalusia, my second high school at this point.

I wasn't just organized or ready when it came to school; I actually put in the work. I took pride in staying on top of things, whether it was a worksheet in class or an assignment due the next day. I'd usually get my work done ahead of time, not because I was trying to impress anyone, but because I genuinely cared about doing things right. I listened in class, stayed focused, and tried to understand what was being taught. It wasn't about being the smartest kid in the room; I was not that kid, but more about showing up and being present in the moments, staying consistent, and doing the job the way I knew it needed to be done.

By the time I hit my senior year, everything felt like it had finally settled, even if just temporarily. I had moved so many times, been in so many schools, and met so many faces that never stuck around long enough to matter. But Elko, despite being in the middle of nowhere, felt oddly like a final lap, a place to exhale. Not because it was glamorous or big or particularly special, but because I finally got to exist in a rhythm without having to pack it up and move on, and that feeling allowed me to fit in because I knew that there was hopefully no more moving.

I was not that much of a social animal, occasionally socializing with my peers on subjects like comics, sports cards, or video games. Outside of those things, I pretty much kept to myself, something that started back in 9th grade when I lived with Dad and Susan.

I had a solid routine back then; one I stuck to without much thought as the days turned into weeks and the weeks into months. I'd wake up each morning, catch the bus to school, sit through my classes, and head home unless my stepmom was able to swing by and pick me up.

Once I got home, I'd head upstairs to our own little haven; just me and Roy, my younger brother. That upstairs floor was like a personal world carved out just for us. I'd spend the time flipping through my comic books or sorting trading cards, losing myself in those familiar routines until it was time to set the table or help out with some chores. Susan had a way of keeping the household running, and being the oldest. I figured it was fair that I pitched in. I didn't mind.

Evenings were simple. After dinner and showers, Roy and I would either fire up the Nintendo for some Tetris or Super Mario, or if the weather was good, we'd hop on our bikes and explore the neighborhood until the sun dipped behind the trees. Sundays were always church days; Baptist services like clockwork; and in the summer, there were usually extra church events that gave us something to do. Looking back, ninth grade felt uneventful, almost like a waiting period. I already knew I'd be moving back in with Mom before too long, so part of me just went through the motions.

That next year, true to plan, Mom and Curt moved back to Alabama from Nevada, and I went to live with them in Andalusia. Roy stayed behind with Dad, and John was still living with his mom. Not long after, Uncle Johnny and my cousin John John made their way to town, too, following a divorce of their own. Ironically, they ended up renting the same trailer we'd lived in back when I first arrived in Andalusia in eighth grade. This time around, things felt different. Mom and Curt had a little more money, and we had a small house tucked away at the end of a dirt road. It wasn't anything fancy, but it was ours, and it felt like a fresh start. We even had our horses that became part of the family from our first adventure to Nevada.

Each morning, I caught a ride to school with the girl next door, Kelly. We were both in 10th grade, but she had a late birthday, so she was actually a little older and already driving. I had a bit of a crush on her; not that I ever said anything; but those rides were one of the few quiet highlights of my day.

School was normal: classes, a little socializing, and a quiet kind of existence. I didn't have many close friends outside of April, who still lived across the street from the old trailer. Most days after school, I'd meet up with my cousin; either lending a hand while he worked on his dad's truck, putting some cherry bomb glass packs on it, or just roaming the woods behind our place, not really looking for anything but time to kill. Once I had my license, I started giving a couple of friends rides to school. I'd usually show up early, park myself in the hallway outside class, and pass the time sketching pages from comic books I liked. Drawing had always come naturally, and even though I didn't talk much, it gave people a reason to notice me. I wasn't outgoing, but I had a few solid connections in each class, most of which stayed never really left the classroom, though there were a few from my art class who I'd actually spend time with outside of school, too.

Some of those closer friends were connections made from our final stretch in Nevada for 11th and 12th grade. Sometimes I would go to my buddy's dad's shop after school since I did not have work right away. It was a quaint little hangout spot that his dad managed on the side while working as a deputy sheriff, which sold sports and comics that all the kids around Elko used to love. It had something for everyone, including comics and cards, as well as 4 or 5 arcade games for a little change of pace. When I got tired of reading and admiring the special edition cards in the glass cases of the shop, I used to kill time by dropping quarters into the games; Mortal Kombat was usually the go-to, sometimes Final Fight if I felt like mixing it up. After that, I'd head back to the house, grab something to eat or crash for a bit, then throw on my work clothes and head out. My job was just around the corner from the card shop, so it made for an easy transition from downtime to clocking in.

At school, things were as monotonous as they could get. However, there were some subjects I actually looked forward to; Art, Photography, and, surprisingly enough, German. It wasn't that I had some grand vision of speaking fluently or traveling to Berlin, but the class had a certain calmness to it. My teacher, Herr Johnson, made it feel less like a lesson and more like a weird little club where you learned how to express everyday things in an entirely new way. Plus, it gave me another excuse to draw. I'd doodle while conjugating verbs or sketch classmates' faces on the margins of my homework. I was always doodling; sometimes comic panels, sometimes just shapes or characters I had half-imagined. It was like my brain could never quite sit still, but the pen helped channel it. The notebook pages became a playground for my thoughts.

Art class was the real safe zone. I wasn't the loudest or the most expressive person in the room, but I didn't need to be when I was there. My work spoke first. A lot of the kids in those classes were kind of on the same wavelength; quiet, thoughtful, mostly just trying to make sense of the world through colors, shadows, and perspective. There was a kid named Chris who loved airbrushing skateboards and another named Jamie who was obsessed with taking black-and-white portraits. We weren't tight like blood, but in that classroom, there was mutual respect. That mattered. It gave me a sense of place when I didn't have much else that grounded me. It wasn't about who was the best artist, but who was honest through their art. We all spoke different creative languages, but we understood one another just the same.

And then there was the theater. I used to work the evening shift for Mr. and Mrs. Larson at the Crystal Movie Theater.

Working at the theater was more than just a paycheck. It gave me structure and a sense of being needed. I wasn't just clocking in; I was trusted. It was my first working role where I had a sense of responsibility. Mr. and Mrs. Larson, who owned the place, were an older couple, kind people who treated the staff like family. Because I was the only guy on the team for the longest time, and the Larsons were old fashioned, I got the later shifts; closing up, breaking down reels in into their canisters, and watching out the windows, making sure the girls got to their cars safely and weren't alone. I had other work to do there as well, building new movies onto a platter for when they would begin or when they would need to be removed. I didn't mind the responsibility. I think, in a lot of ways, I craved it. It made me feel like I had a role that actually meant something. Having people depend on me made me stand taller.

I got pretty good at threading and splicing film, too. There's a rhythm to it, like piecing together a big puzzle. You would open those heavy cans, each one carrying two or three reels like some sacred relic, and carefully feed them into the platter system. It was mechanical and precise; one wrong move, and you'd have film wrapped around the floor like a spaghetti monster. But when it worked, it was smooth and satisfying. You could hear the hum of the projector from the back booth, echoing across empty aisles while the audience stayed glued to the screen. Sometimes, I'd linger a few minutes to catch the first scenes of a new movie before heading back to clean or get ready for the next reel swap.

There was one evening I was cleaning up, while John John, Roy, and John were walking around waiting for me to drive us all home after work. They apparently decided to go by the liquor store and found some old guy to buy them some Zimas. I'm not sure how they pulled it off since John John was only 17 and Roy was barely 15. They then put the Zimas in the back of my Toyota pickup and came inside, hanging out, having already knocked a few back. I snuck them into a movie; it might have been Jurassic Park, I think, when they met this girl and her friends. After it was over, I noticed they had all been drinking. I was kind of pissed. I didn't want to get caught and get in trouble. Anyway, after I jumped their shit, I was breaking down one of the movies and turned the lights in the theater off when I heard someone yell to turn them back on.

I looked out the projector window and saw them down there with one of the girls. I ran downstairs and was asking what the hell was going on when John said, "Watch, man."

I sat down, and one of the girls started doing a striptease right in front of me. Talk about a crazy evening at work. Normally, it was quiet and boring, not at all like that night.

After closing, the drive home down I-80 was quiet. Sometimes eerily so. Nevada nights weren't like Alabama nights. There weren't any chirping crickets or tree frogs humming in the background. Just wind and space and headlights slicing through the desert black. The house we were renting was on the Skrabo Ranch, sat way out from the town center, so by the time I got home, it was dead quiet. No lights from neighbors, no city glow on the horizon. Just the house sitting there, like a tiny island in a sea of nothing. There was an odd peace in that isolation. The vastness of the land around us made even the biggest worries feel smaller somehow.

My room was upstairs, small and cozy. I didn't mind that it wasn't big; I had my comics, my sketch pads, and a little boom box radio that helped fill the space. Some nights, I'd crash immediately; other nights, I'd lie there with the ceiling fan spinning slowly above me, thinking about all the places I'd been. About the friends I'd had and the ones who faded into the background like old photographs. That room, though modest, became a place to reflect, to rewind, and sometimes, to just vanish. I even had an old red lamp that hung from a chain, gaudy as hell; it was an old brothel lamp.

The weekends were a bit more arduous, not that I minded. In fact, I looked forward to it. It was a fun way to start the day before I clocked into work. I spent a lot of that time with a small group of friends who lived nearby in the same mining company condominiums we used to live in when we first moved to Nevada. We didn't need much to entertain ourselves; just some open space and a little imagination. Sometimes, we'd hike through Lamoille Canyon, a rugged stretch in the Ruby Mountains that felt like a different world compared to the dusty flats around us. There wasn't always a plan; we just knew we'd end up somewhere away from everything else, making our own kind of fun the way bored teenagers do.

Despite all the movement in my life, the inconsistency, the stops and starts, I never really felt lonely. Maybe that was because I didn't expect much permanence from people. Or maybe it was because I learned how to be good at my own company. Having art and stories and the ability to create something out of nothing gave me an escape that didn't rely on anyone else. I didn't need a huge circle of friends or a bunch of parties. I just needed a pencil and a little space to breathe. And that was more than enough on most days.

Of course, some friendships last longer than others. April was probably the most consistent one. Even when we weren't in the same classes or even the same neighborhood, we always picked back up as if no time had passed. There was something comforting about that kind of friendship; no drama, no pressure, just someone who got it. We didn't need to talk every day, but we knew each other's stories well enough to fill in the blanks when we did. She had a quiet strength, and maybe that's why we understood each other so well, because silence didn't scare us. We eventually lost contact and never saw each other again, though.

Then there was John John; my cousin, my shadow, my brother-in-everything-but-blood. Having him out in Elko with me was like getting a piece of home transplanted into the desert. We grew up thick as thieves back in the South, and being reunited as teenagers just made that bond stronger. That's the thing about childhood friendships; they don't need time to warm up. They're always ready, like an old sweatshirt you throw on after a long day. Being with him reminded me of who I was before all the moves, before all the growing up.

I spent a lot of time thinking about what came next. I knew I wasn't going to stay in Elko forever, and I knew college wasn't going to be the path for me right out of the gate. We didn't have the money for that. Drawing was my passion, sure; but it never felt like a career path back then. It felt more like a hobby that kept me sane, not something I could build a future on. But the Navy? That was a certainty. Even before I hit double digits, I had already made that decision. The thought of wearing that uniform, of being part of something bigger than myself, gave me direction when little else did.

Some kids dream about going to college or becoming astronauts or actors. I dreamed about serving. I dreamed about structure, honor, and escape, all wrapped into one. The Navy offered direction, a straight line in a life that had mostly been a zigzag. And with every move, every relocation, every time I had to say goodbye to people and places, that dream only got clearer. It wasn't about running away; it was about heading toward something.

At home, the dynamic between Mom and Curt was good. Better than I think most people expected, considering all the moving and uncertainty. Curt was solid. A guy who worked hard, didn't complain much, and treated Mom with the kind of respect she hadn't always gotten before. Our little trio had a rhythm; work, school, chores, repeat. We weren't flashy or loud, but we made it work. Stability doesn't always come with big fanfare; sometimes, it just means having someone to rely on every day.

Mom, despite everything she had been through; divorce, raising kids across different states, financial hardship; never once made me feel like we were lacking. Even when we lived for months in that tiny motel room in Elko before our housing opened up, she made it feel like home. There was love there. And I think that kind of foundation mattered more than any square footage or paycheck. She had an uncanny ability to make any space feel warm, and that warmth carried us through the roughest patches.

We didn't talk much about the past; about the divorce or the reasons why everything unfolded the way it did. But you didn't need to say things out loud to understand them. I saw how hard she worked. I saw the sacrifices she made. I remember her giving up everything; literally walking away from the house, the furniture, the washer and dryer; just so she could have a fresh start. That stuck with me. It showed me that starting over doesn't mean failure. Sometimes, it means choosing peace over comfort.

Before Mom met Curt, life was lean. We lived in low-income housing, scraping by on what little she managed to earn. It wasn't until years later, closer to the present than to those early days, that her sacrifice really hit me. We were going through a box when we came across one of her old Social Security statements and saw that after the divorce from my dad, she was only bringing in four digits a year. That number stuck with me. It put into perspective just how much she had let go of without asking for anything in return. She walked away with just the trunk and the table my grandma had given her. That kind of quiet strength said a lot about who she was; and it shaped how I saw things too.

By contrast, ninth grade felt like the one "normal" year of high school, mostly because I was living with my dad and Susan, my stepmom. They were both doing well financially, so we never really wanted for anything. We shopped at the outlets in San Destin and wore name-brand clothes; Nike, Guess, Reebok, Z-Cavaricci; and didn't have to think much about whether we could afford them. It was a different kind of life, one with its comforts and routines, and in a way, it made things feel stable. But I could never ignore the stark difference between that life and the one my mom was living. With Dad, there was plenty. With Mom, there was effort. There was a sacrifice. And I think it was through that contrast that I learned how to appreciate what I had on a deeper level.

At one point, my dad even offered me a car; the 1990 Ford Taurus he and Susan drove. He told me it was mine if I chose to stay in DeFuniak Springs with them. It was a tempting offer, especially for a teenager who didn't yet have much. But I kept thinking about Mom; how she was alone now, how Roy had decided to stay with Dad, and how she had just married Curt. I felt like she needed someone in her corner, and I figured if it wasn't going to be Roy, then it should be me.

When they were still in Nevada, Curt had a steady job, and things seemed alright. But after they moved back to Alabama for my tenth-grade year, both he and Mom ended up working at the cotton gin in Andalusia; the same place where they'd first met. It wasn't glamorous work, but it was honest, and it was enough to get by. Looking back, that decision; to be with her instead of staying with my dad; was a turning point. It meant giving up a few comforts, sure. But it also meant growing up and understanding that sometimes doing the right thing isn't about what's easy. It's about who needs you most.

When people ask if I had a comfortable life, I remember these times we went through, and I never know quite how to answer. Materially? Maybe not always. There were times we had to stretch groceries or skip certain luxuries. But emotionally? I felt secure. I felt like I mattered. And I think that's more than a lot of kids get. The money stuff; sure, it shaped how I see the world today. I don't hoard it; I don't obsess over it. But I do respect it. I spend on the things that matter, and I make memories without guilt. Because I remember what it was like to have less and still feel full.

Looking back, those high school years weren't traditional. I didn't have the same best friend all four years, a locker I decorated every semester, or a prom date I'd marry ten years later. What I had instead were fragments; snapshots of different lives stitched together by a constant search for purpose. And while that might sound sad to some people, I think it made me more adaptable, more curious, and more real.

I learned how to say goodbye. I learned how to be alone without being lonely. I learned how to take care of people without being asked. And I learned that it's okay not to have all the answers at 17, or any age really.

I didn't know exactly what would happen after graduation. But I knew this much: The Navy was coming. The world was waiting. And I was ready to meet it on my own terms.

Chapter 7
Following the Passion

The year was 1993, and after years of adjusting, I was finally settling down without any looming threat of moving within a month or two. At the time, I was a senior at Elko High School and had grown quite accustomed to my school, the people, and life, as this was the longest I had been at a school throughout my life. Elko was the place where I grew most as a student because life allowed me the time to grow and adjust there.

Settling down in Elko provided me with opportunities that I was not allowed to consider previously due to the constant moving and adapting to new environments. Since there was continuity in my life in Elko, I was more social and outgoing, albeit still a bit shy. However, that didn't stop me this time, and I made more than a couple of friends. These bonds were a major contributing factor to my growth as a student at Elko High.

Although I was making friends in high school, now that I was more accustomed to my life in Elko, I wanted more. I wanted to pursue my future, which was the Navy. I had always wanted to join the Navy and serve my country just like how my grandfather did, cementing the history our family had with this branch of the armed forces. I made the formal decision during my junior year in Elko High School, with my parents signing my consent form since I was still a minor, and admitting me into the DEP, also known as the Delayed Entry Program. Signing up for this program allowed me to get into a contract with the Navy early on without having to go on active duty right away, allowing me up to a year of delay, which was just enough time for me to get done with high school.

As far as signing the consent form was concerned, when I told my parents my desire to join the Navy and serve the country, they did not try to dissuade me in any way. In fact, they were incredibly proud that I was following in the footsteps of my grandfather and promised to support me in any way they could. I was finally at the starting line, proud and determined to serve my country in the Navy.

One of my biggest motivators for specifically wanting to join the Navy, was the deep family legacy we had with the branch. On my dad's side, my grandfather served during World War II, on the USS Alabama - a mighty battleship that saw action in both the Atlantic and the Pacific theaters - before retiring as a Warrant Officer following many years. Between his service, one of my uncles on my dad's side, and my grandpa's time in his Navy blues, these men cast long shadows of pride and discipline over my childhood.

A visit to Battleship Memorial Park in Mobile, Alabama, where the Alabama now rests as a museum, brought Grandpa's service to life in a powerful way. As I stood on the same steel decks he once walked, Grandma Evans on my dad's side, shared details of his time in the Navy. That moment connected the dots for me, anchoring my choice to follow in his footsteps. His service wasn't just a story from the past; it was a part of my foundation.

Although Shirley Mae did eventually find the strength to leave that toxic marriage behind, the memories still remain, good and bad. Her marriage to my maternal grandpa reminded me that while military service brought honor, the lives surrounding that service were often just as complex, messy, and deeply human.

Not only my parents, but my siblings and friends were also incredibly proud of me for doing this, and I even inspired some of them to join as well. Some of my closest friends are those who began their journey motivated by my actions and enrolled in the Marines, along with my brother, who eventually joined the National Guard after passing out of college.

However, there were a couple of friends who were a bit skeptical of the idea, urging me to think of a backup or a fallback just in case, but they were soon reassured and supportive of my decision once I told them that I had a plan. I didn't tell them that just for the sake of reassurance and peace of mind, but I actually had a well-thought-out plan that covered all bases.

While understanding the eligibility criteria to get enlisted and apply for the DEP program, I touched on a lot of different topics to prepare certain precautions just in case, one of which was the Montgomery GI Bill, which was the last resort in the case that I had to leave the Navy, which would provide me with a financial cushion after college just in case the Navy didn't work out for me, the likelihood of which was incredibly low, but still present. No matter what happened, I knew that I would push through the adversities, and the fact that I had a solid, goal-oriented plan for my future at this age made me incredibly confident in the steps I was taking.

While the Navy was my first choice and my passion, that didn't mean it was my only dream. I had other aspirations as well, and I always felt like, if, due to some reason, I had to drop out of the Navy or it didn't work out, I would be some sort of scientist or a lawyer. I had a knack for debating just about anything, which naturally fed the lawyer fantasy. And I was always drawn to science, not just the classroom kind, but the curious, odd bits of knowledge that most people didn't bother to remember.

Still, none of those ideas ever fully stuck. What did stick was the idea of the Navy, not just as a career path but as a way to figure out what I really wanted to do with my life. I'd already moved around enough within the U.S. to know I wanted to see more outside the country, across oceans, in places most people only read about.

The Navy offered that chance. It was also a way to

connect with something bigger than myself, something rooted in my family's past. That legacy, along with my restlessness to see the world, made joining the Navy feel like the right step forward, not just to serve but to grow.

Deciding to join the Navy wasn't some spur-of-the-moment thing; I approached it like a mission. I dug into every detail I could find, asked every question that came to mind, and made sure my mom knew I was serious, not just chasing another teenage impulse. At the time, we were living in Elko, Nevada; a quiet town with big skies and not much else. The nearest Navy recruiting office was five hours away in Salt Lake City, Utah, which might as well have been across the country. Luckily, since Elko was in their area of responsibility, recruiters would occasionally come through the high school. That's where I first crossed paths with Steve Canale, the recruiter who'd eventually help steer me through the whole process. Once I committed, things picked up quickly. I rode with Steve to Salt Lake to fill out paperwork at his office, then spent the night in a hotel so I could be up early the next morning for my appointment at MEPS; the Military Entrance Processing Station.

That day still lives pretty clearly in my memory. I remember having a glass of orange juice with breakfast, which seemed innocent enough at the time. Turned out, not the best idea. The sugar from the juice threw off my urinalysis, showing abnormal levels and triggering a few raised eyebrows. That led to several hours of waiting around and drinking water until I could test clean. Not exactly the smooth start I'd pictured. Then came the surprise revelation that I had flat feet; something I'd never noticed since they never caused me pain or gave me a reason to think twice. But the Navy needed documentation, so they took polaroid photos of my feet for a Bureau of Medicine and Surgery waiver. I can still remember the weird feeling of propping my feet up on a desk while someone snapped photos like it was a passport shoot for my arches.

Just when I thought I was in the clear, I made an offhand comment about the time I almost had brain surgery. That didn't go over well. The cyst I'd been evaluated for years earlier had never caused issues, but the fact that it hadn't been disclosed earlier set off another round of paperwork and medical reviews.

About that, when I was 16 on vacation with Dad, Susan, Roy, David, and Becky, we were stopped overnight in Oregon at a hotel. I woke up at something like 2 in the morning with a nose bleed, and while standing trying to stop the bleeding, I must have passed out. I woke up what after what may have been a few minutes, still not really sure, but my ribs hurt, I had dried blood on my chest and I had pissed myself. I was embarrassed so I never spoke of it until sometime in the winter. I nonchalantly brought it up to mom who freaked out. Next thing I know we were driving to the Children's' Hospital in Salt Lake City where I was getting all kinds of tests done. I was getting poked and prodded; it was all unpleasant. After many scans, they found out I had a condition called septo optic dysplasia.

Apparently, my bad eyesight was connected to this. I also found out a membrane, the septum pellucidum, that divides the left and right sides of our brains was missing in mine. They also found a small cyst in the cerebral aqueduct of my brain. It was apparently benign, but if it grew or caused any blockage, I would have had a risk of a hydrocephalus. This could have been the reason I had a seizure and passed out on vacation. Doctors said it could have been a once in a lifetime incident, but also said it could happen again and could lead to serious results, and possibly kill me.

I was scheduled for brain surgery to remove the cyst. While I was being tested, I mentioned the frequent nosebleeds I would get, so they decided to go ahead and cauterize the vessels in my nose with acid. To this day, it was the most horrible pain I have experienced, and my pain tolerance has always been exceptionally high, and it smelled like bananas. The night before surgery, we got a visit from the surgeons, cancelling the surgery. To this day I am not sure exactly why or what happened to lead to the cancellation. I never really got a straight answer from my parents other than the risk was too high. So apparently, I still have this cyst in my brain, I guess?

We had to track down old records, get statements from doctors, and prove that I was medically fit to serve. It dragged everything out far longer than I expected. But eventually, in

December of 1993, everything was squared away. I stood in a quiet room, raised my right hand, and swore into the Delayed Entry Program. It felt like a door opening; one I had pushed through entirely on my own.

After I finally swore in, my recruiter, Steve Canale, put me on a Greyhound bus to make the return trip home. Sure, it was a straight shot on I-80, but it felt like the longest ride of my life. I sat there staring out the window, exhausted and wired at the same time, with every stop dragging the ride out even further. That was my first; and hopefully last; experience with Greyhound. Every in-person task, every form that had to be signed face-to-face, meant another full day lost to travel. It tested my patience, but it also showed me what persistence really looked like. I had started this journey on my own, and no number of setbacks was going to stop me from finishing it.

I would eventually transition into the world as an adult to serve in the U.S. Navy.

Chapter 8
First Tour in the Navy

Normally, it is very unlikely for your family to take the news that you are joining the military well. After all, the open seas are unpredictable, and be it other militaries or the perils of the ocean, there are many elements that are a threat to your life, and your parents do not wish for you to accelerate the process of dying by signing up for the military.

However, thankfully, this was not an issue for my parents. In fact, they were proud of the decision I had made. As mentioned before, I had a history with this branch of the military, so my parents understood what it meant to me.

No matter how much support I got, it doesn't mean that my time in the Navy was a walk in the park. Throughout the journey, I will say that it was fun learning how to become a leader and serving in the Navy, but it would always have its challenges.

When I left for the Navy, my first destination was Recruit Training Command in Great Lakes, Illinois, commonly referred to as RTC. It was a world far removed from anything I had ever experienced. Though I was technically an adult, it didn't feel like freedom in any way. We weren't allowed to leave the base for eight weeks, and every hour of every day was scheduled. I was assigned to Company 263, Division 2, and our Company Commanders were DC1 Tender and BM1 Wilde. They weren't overly hands-on but provided us with a Plan of the Day that spelled out everything from when to wake up, when and where to eat, study Naval and military history, and when we trained for shipboard firefighting or took physical readiness tests. Everything was laid out in military precision, from reveille to taps.

The topics ranged from naval history and leadership to first aid, seamanship, and knot-tying. Graduation brought liberty, and we finally got a taste of freedom with the chance to go into Chicago, walk the streets, eat real food, and breathe as civilians for a day.

Navy boot camp photo.

After boot camp, I was assigned to Hull Maintenance Technician (HT) 'A' School in Philadelphia. The school was located at the end of Broad Street, one of the two main arteries in the city. As someone raised in small-town America, having the entire 13-mile stretch of Broad Street at my doorstep felt like being dropped into another world. The training was comprehensive and intense. We learned stick, MIG, and TIG welding, sheet metal work, pipe-fitting, fiberglass repair, woodworking, and in-depth firefighting and damage control. To a degree, everything was self-paced, and while some could test out of portions if they had prior experience, most of us, including myself, came in green. I had been working in a movie theater before joining the Navy, so this was all new to me.

Outside of class, Philadelphia became my playground. South Street, with its eclectic storefronts and gritty charm, became a regular haunt. Tower Records was a favorite, and I spent a lot of time people-watching and wandering without a destination. I loved going to the UA Theater on Columbus Boulevard, partly because of my love for movies but also because that's where I first saw Erin. She worked there, and from the moment I noticed her, something about her stood out. We exchanged glances, and I kept showing up, hoping for another encounter. I was too shy to make the first move, but my buddy Kevin, whom I met in HT school, wasn't. He noticed her, too, and eventually asked her out first.

Kevin, I, and another friend, Finn, started hanging out with Erin regularly. She became our informal guide to Philly, showing us around and introducing us to her city. Erin was born and raised in South Philadelphia, and she had that local pride. Despite Kevin dating her, there was an unspoken connection between Erin and me. I'd lend her my favorite CDs and underline lyrics in the booklets to send subtle messages. She noticed. She was a singer and a writer, so words meant something to her. Kevin knew how I felt about her even before he met her, which made the whole situation feel murky. Still, we all remained close.

When our HT school wrapped up in February 1995, 18 of us unexpectedly received orders to the same base, Navy Submarine Base in Groton, Connecticut. Normally, HTs would be assigned to ships, but we were placed in Repair Division 1, or R1, where we worked in different shops: Ship fitting, pipefitting, lagging, sheet metal, and tool control. Kevin and I became roommates in the barracks, while Shun, another friend from school, roomed a few floors down with Gary. Reyna, Gandeza, and a few others from our school also ended up in Groton, also known as "Rotten Groton," and the destination for my first tour, which lasted for around two very eventful years.

Kevin and I would still drive down to Philly occasionally to see Erin. Even after he and Erin broke up, we visited her, and it was always as a group. But one day, things blew up. Kevin had twisted something I said about my feelings for Erin, telling her that I claimed we had been secretly together. That couldn't have been further from the truth. Erin confronted me, furious. I had no idea what she was even talking about until I dug into it. I hopped on a train to Chestnut Hill, where she was attending college, and walked through the snow from the station to meet her. We talked, and I explained everything. Kevin had lied. Things got better between us, though not completely, so we were not the same for a while. I decided to try and move on from Erin and look elsewhere.

That led to the beginning of way more adventures in the near future than I would ever expect.

The beginning was during a New Year's Eve visit to Nevada, I went to a party hosted by Keith and Theresa, friends of my stepdad, Curt. There was this girl who kept bringing me drinks. I had never met her, but she was cute, and it was a fun evening. Drink after drink, she was always there. After drinking a bit, she invited me to a bar for the ball drop, which, in hindsight, as I say those words, almost seems ironic. After being denied entry into the bar since I wasn't 21 yet, I waited outside, bummed out, and shit faced. Eventually, I left with the same girl who brought me to the bar, but instead of heading back to Keith and Theresa's house, we went to her place. Since I was already a bit tipsy from drinks earlier in the evening, I thought, *why not.*

When we got back, things escalated quickly. We continued drinking, and before long, she initiated sex. I was still a virgin, heavily intoxicated, and I honestly didn't know what I was doing. I was physically there, but barely; mentally and emotionally, I was detached because I was so drunk and exhausted. I eventually passed out and called my stepdad the next morning to come pick me up. I was embarrassed and ashamed. That's not something you might hear a guy say anything about after a night like that, but that's not how I envisioned my first time. It wasn't consensual in a meaningful sense; I didn't have the clarity or sobriety to know what I was doing. It left me with a feeling of regret and discomfort that stayed with me for a long time.

The one thing I gained, was a little more confidence. After Christmas and the New Year was in full swing, back in Connecticut, my friends and I met three girls at the Crystal Mall. They invited us to a house party in Putnam. I clicked with one of them, and we crashed at her place after the party. Though nothing happened that first night, there was something about her that lingered with me. We started talking more, and soon enough, there was a real connection. I would be her first sexual partner. It was new territory for me. Before long, we were dating, things moved quickly and she moved in with me.

The relationship was fast and intense. Suddenly, I went from someone barely comfortable with physical intimacy to being in a relationship defined by it. It was overwhelming and exciting. For a while, it felt good to be wanted, to feel like I was finally experiencing the closeness I had missed in earlier years. But the intensity became suffocating. We were always together, and as close as we were physically and emotionally, things began to fray at the edges.

That's when I found out about the other guy. He worked a few stores down from where she was employed at the mall. She had told me she wasn't going to a cornfield party one night, saying she had to work. But eventually she admitted she went with the other guy from the mall, and she kissed him. It crushed me. It was the first time I had ever been cheated on, and it hit like a truck. I remember feeling blindsided; not just by her actions but by how quickly something I thought was solid had unraveled. The betrayal was sharp, and it came right when I was already at my lowest.

Around the same time, I got word from the Navy that I'd been overpaid. I didn't even know what I'd done wrong, but the result was devastating; my paychecks garnished for repayment. I was sinking fast. I remember looking at my bank account and feeling panic rising in my chest, like a Redd Sanford moment. I'd always been the responsible one, the guy who didn't make waves; but now it felt like my life was slipping out of my control. I couldn't even afford the basics. I felt like a failure.

My Master Chief must've seen all of the burden weighing on me. He pulled me aside one day and said, "You need to take some time. Get out of here. Clear your head." I had been given backpay for the funds when he told me to request and take leave, and I took it without hesitation. I needed a break.

I hit the road to visit my dad in Florida, just trying to put some distance between me and the mess. On the way, I called Erin. We hadn't really spoken in a while; not since everything between us had gone sideways. But I missed her. I missed what she represented: Something pure, something real that never had a chance to become something bigger. To my surprise, she picked up. Even more surprising, she and her Grandma offered to let me stay with them in Philly.

Being back with Erin was surreal. There was still a spark between us. We talked, really talked, in ways I hadn't been able to with anyone in a long time. We kissed for the first time. It was about reconnection, about something unresolved finally being brought into the light.

When I asked her to come with me to Florida, it felt spontaneous but right. We drove down together, just the two of us, and I started to feel hope again. After a few days, it was time to go back to Connecticut. On the way back, something came over me, I pulled off on the side of the road, I asked her to go with me to Nevada. My mom was there, and I hadn't told her we were coming. I didn't care. I just needed to keep moving, needed something different. Erin said yes again. I didn't have a plan. I just couldn't go back to the Navy yet. I couldn't face the consequences, couldn't face the uniform, couldn't face myself. Erin didn't flinch. She just nodded and said, "Okay."

That "okay" meant more than she probably knew. It

meant I wasn't alone.

It was a cross country road trip full of adventure and exploring. It was freedom on the road, and I suspended the idea of responsibility for a brief moment in time. We showed up at my mom's house unannounced. I don't know what I was expecting; maybe understanding, maybe concern; but what I do know is I was desperate to be seen, to be grounded again. I was not just running away from my recent relationship or the Navy or my bank account. I was running from this version of myself I didn't recognize anymore; a version that felt broken and lost and unsure of its place in the world.

Erin didn't just come with me; she brought me calm in that moment. I didn't know what came next, but with her, at least I didn't feel like I was alone.

When I left Groton, I wasn't planning to disappear. But I also wasn't ready to go back.

I was officially UA; unauthorized absence. That label alone carried a weight I couldn't fully grasp at the time. I had always been the dependable one; the one people could rely on to do the right thing, follow the rules, and show up. But this time, I didn't show up. I vanished. I did not tell the Navy; I did not call my command; I just left. My dad panicked and filed for state police to put out an APB up and down the East Coast where we were supposed to be driving. My mom had no idea where I was. Even Erin's father was calling around, trying to understand what the hell was happening. It wasn't like me. And that's what scared everyone the most.

But the truth is; I didn't know who "me" was anymore.

In the middle of the chaos, there was Erin. She was the one person who didn't demand anything from me. She didn't ask why I was breaking down and didn't push me to explain my decisions. She was just there with a quiet steadiness I hadn't realized I needed so badly. We had history; this unspoken thread that had been woven between us since our earliest encounters in Philly. Back then, I was too shy to say how I felt. Too late to act when my friend made the first move. But now, with the walls down and the world crumbling behind me, it was just us.

It was the first time I didn't have to pretend to be strong or have it all figured out. She loved me where I was, not where I thought I was supposed to be.

Erin and I talked about getting married, not because of tradition or romance or timing, but because we both felt like we were clinging to something real in a world that had gone sideways. We believed, maybe foolishly, that a marriage certificate might soften the blow when I eventually went back to face the music. So, we did it. On July 24th, at the Elko County Courthouse. My mom, Curt, Keith, and Theresa stood by as witnesses. It wasn't some fairytale wedding, but it was ours. It was raw, honest, and born of mutual need and deep, complicated love.

That day meant something to me. For the first time in what felt like months, I felt like I was choosing something for *me*, not for duty, not out of guilt or pressure, but because I wanted a future with her.

Twenty-eight days after going to UA, I returned to Groton. My seabag slung over my shoulder, heart pounding, stomach in knots; I was ready for it. Ready to face restriction, punishment, Captain's Mast, whatever they had in store. I had accepted my fate. But when I walked in… nothing. No reprimand. No chewing out. No paperwork. Just silence.

For months, no one said a word.

On the outside, that might seem like a relief; but it wasn't. It left me in this strange purgatory. I was free, but not really. I was back, but not whole. It was like I was waiting for a shoe to drop that never did. I lived in a state of quiet anxiety, pretending everything was fine when nothing really was.

Still, I had Erin. And even though our world was shaky, she gave me something to hold on to. She was my lifeline. Loving her during that time was the most honest thing I had. And in a life where I was beginning to question everything; my decisions, my career, my identity; *that* was the only thing that felt undeniably right.

Eventually, my moment came. Another sailor had recently

been caught for being UA; pulled over by state police for speeding in his Corvette; and once that hit the chain of command, the Navy could no longer ignore my own absence. It was only a matter of time before I was called in. I had been walking on eggshells every day, knowing I was a loose thread waiting to be pulled.

They called me to Captain's Mast, the Navy's version of non-judicial punishment. I showed up with my full seabag, every uniform packed meticulously, because when you stand in front of the Commanding Officer at Mast, you don't get to go home first if it doesn't go your way. If you're found guilty, you're confined immediately. No civilian clothes. No personal space. Just orders and a rack to sleep on in the restriction barracks.

Standing there, I felt the weight of every bad decision I'd made in the past month pressing into my shoulders like lead. I expected 45 days of restriction to base, meaning I'd be confined to the barracks under constant supervision and 45 days of half pay. And even that would be a gift compared to what they *could* give me. Erin was pregnant; we had nowhere to go and no support system to fall back on. I was married, broke, and terrified of losing it all.

When the CO looked me in the eye and asked why I did what I did, I didn't make excuses. I told the truth. I explained that Erin had no home if I were confined. We had gotten married during that time because I needed to believe I was building something good out of the chaos. I didn't run out of selfishness; I ran because I was broken and didn't know how to ask for help.

He listened. Then he spoke.

He suspended the punishment; *all of it*; for 90 days.

That meant no restriction. No loss of pay. But it wasn't forgiveness; it was a warning, razor-thin and ice-cold.

"If I wake up on the wrong side of the bed tomorrow," he said, eyes locked on mine, "or if you mess up even once, I'll bring you right back here. And you *will* receive the full punishment. Do you understand me, shipmate?"

"Yes, sir," I replied. There wasn't an ounce of fight left in my voice; just respect, fear, and a quiet flood of relief.

Walking out of that room didn't feel like freedom. It felt like parole. I was still wearing the uniform and still showing up to work, but I knew the eyes were on me now. One misstep, one late arrival, one wrong word; and I'd be back in front of that CO, but next time, there'd be no leniency.

I returned to Erin afterwards, not as the same man who walked out a month earlier. I had crossed a line and been yanked back by the thinnest thread of mercy. And now, I had something even heavier to carry: the knowledge that I had been *given* grace; and if I blew it, there would be no one to blame but myself.

But Erin was still waiting for me. Pregnant, nervous, but proud. I had made it back. Now, I just had to hold it together.

We were already living with Shun and his girlfriend, Paula, a stripper he met at a club. Living with them was chaotic. Drugs, arguments, and instability ruled the apartment. Erin and I eventually found our own place on Crystal Avenue; though most people around town didn't call it that. Locals knew it as "Crack Avenue," a grim nickname that told you everything you needed to know about the neighborhood. The rent was cheap, and that was all we could afford. The apartment wasn't much; bare bones, dim lighting, a mattress on the floor for a bed, and a mismatched set of furniture we had picked up off the curb from someone's house in Navy housing. But it was ours. After the instability of bouncing around between barracks, friends' apartments, and family homes, just having a door we could lock and call our own felt like a small piece of freedom. A refuge.

But it didn't last long.

Erin's younger brother came to live with us not long after we settled in. He had run into some trouble back in Philly, and Erin; being Erin; wanted to help him get a fresh start. We found him a job at the Navy Exchange, but that didn't last. He was restless, aimless, and, more than anything, a disruption. The tension in the apartment rose fast. Erin was pregnant, dealing with hormonal shifts and the emotional weight of carrying our child. Her younger brother, still immature and reckless, constantly stirred things up. He'd pick fights, make smart-ass remarks, and challenge both of us over nothing. It felt like walking through a minefield every time I came home, not knowing what went down while I was at work.

And I was under pressure, too. After nearly losing my career over my UA incident, I was hanging by a thread. One mistake; *one*; and the suspended punishment would drop on me like a hammer. I was trying to keep everything together, trying to stay responsible, trying to breathe; but inside, I was drowning. Bills were tight, the apartment felt more claustrophobic by the day, and every argument between Erin and her brother chipped away at my sanity.

Then, one night, everything changed.

I came home late, exhausted, ready to collapse. Erin was already in bed. I slipped in next to her and reached under her pillow, searching for the cool side. My hand hit something cold, hard and metallic. I pulled it out; a butter knife? I looked at her, confused.

She looked back at me, dead serious.

"Aaron, I'm scared of him, he's fucking crazy" she said in her South Philly accent.

That moment hit me like a punch to the chest. I didn't

have words. Erin; this woman I had run away with, married, and was building a life with; was sleeping with a dull knife under her pillow because she didn't feel safe in our own home. I felt ashamed. Powerless. Angry.

It was supposed to be a safe place. I had promised her that, at the very least. And now she couldn't even close her eyes without protection.

I lay there next to her that night, wide awake, staring at the ceiling, the knife resting on the nightstand. Every sound in the apartment made me flinch. I realized that our little slice of freedom had become another kind of prison. The stress of being young, broke, married, and responsible for a life I didn't yet know how to manage was tearing at the seams of everything I believed I could hold together.

I was just a kid trying to be a man. Trying to protect the woman I loved. And I was failing.

The next morning, I told Erin we had to figure something out. Her brother couldn't stay, not like this. She agreed; but the damage had been done. That image of the butter knife stayed with me. A symbol of how fragile our world had become. And how quickly the weight of life could turn hope into fear.

Erin's pregnancy wasn't easy from the start. Early on, we were told it was high-risk, and there was a strong possibility that our daughter might be born with Down Syndrome. The news shook us both; me more than I let on. We were just kids ourselves, suddenly having to think about genetic disorders, medical specialists, and what kind of future we could provide for a child who might need lifelong support.

We started traveling to Yale University Medical Center, where they ran a battery of tests. We sat through long consultations and ultrasounds, and eventually even met with support groups; families with children already navigating the life we were preparing ourselves for. It was overwhelming. Not because we didn't want her; but because we *did*; and we were scared we wouldn't be enough.

Amid all of this, I was selected for new orders. I was being transferred to the USS *John F. Kennedy* (CV-67), stationed in Mayport, Florida. At the time, we were told it was a "training carrier"; supposedly a ship that didn't deploy. I clung to that detail like a lifeline. Erin and I told ourselves we could make it work and not having to go to sea, that I would have shore stability and be close enough to be there when the baby came. It was a comforting lie we both wanted to believe.

But then came the gut punch; just weeks after checking in to my new command, they announced we were deploying. And not in a few months; *in less than four weeks.* The day I reported aboard was my 21st birthday. While most people of that age were going out, drinking, and celebrating, I was boarding an aircraft carrier, preparing to leave the country, and leaving behind a wife in her final months of pregnancy. It wasn't a celebration; it was a countdown to departure.

With no home of our own in Florida yet and no time to find one before I left, Erin went to stay with my dad and stepmom in DeFuniak Springs. It made sense at the time. My dad was supportive and respected Erin. But my stepmom; she was a different story. From the very beginning, things felt off. Erin told me how she tried to make the best of it, even while very pregnant and in a house that didn't feel like hers. But my stepmom's behavior turned from cold to openly hostile. She started making passive-aggressive remarks about Erin's friends, especially those who were culturally different, Black, or Asian. She was more worried about what it would look like having diverse people coming and going. Erin was stunned. Hurt. Alone in a strange house with people who were supposed to help her feel safe, but instead made her feel judged and unwanted.

The stress started to wear on her quickly. She was nearly nine months pregnant, alone with no husband, no real allies in the house, and constantly on edge. It was supposed to be a place where she could rest while I was gone. Instead, it became another weight on her already burdened shoulders. My dad was kind, but he worked off shore two weeks at a time, and when he wasn't around, she was left to navigate the relationship with my stepmother's comments and cold stares.

One day, without warning, Erin packed her things, walked out the door, and boarded a Greyhound bus bound for

Philadelphia. No one knew where she had gone. She didn't tell my dad. She didn't tell me. The only person who knew was my brother Roy. She just *left*. It wasn't until much later that I found out what had happened, and it broke something in me. I had left her in a place that hurt her. I thought I was doing the right thing, making arrangements to set her up with my family. I had tried to convince her to go back to Philly to be with her friends and family for the rest of her pregnancy. I agreed to her request for her to stay, but in truth, I hadn't seen the full picture. She was drowning in isolation and prejudice. I was halfway around the world, blind to the fact of what was going on, but I was acutely aware of one thing: I was missing everything.

I spent that deployment trying to keep my head above water; sending money home, working long hours underway, and trying to imagine what it would be like to be a father. I called home with prepaid Sailor Phone cards, 20 minutes at a time, trying to reach Erin. Trying to feel something other than guilt and distance. I didn't even know when my daughter was born. I found out weeks later, secondhand, through a Red Cross message. Her name was Kathleen. I wasn't there for her birth. I wasn't there for Erin when she needed me most.

And part of me still carries that, and always will.

Deployment on the *USS John F. Kennedy* was supposed to be manageable; at least, that's what we were told. Of course, we learned that was not true very quickly. What followed was months of sailing through international waters, stopping in ports like Haifa, Dubai, Marseille; places we were excited to see. Most of the guys I served with spent their free time exploring, going on tours, and enjoying their time overseas. They bought souvenirs, took photos, went out drinking, and lived for the stories they'd tell back home.

I didn't do much of that at all.

I sent almost all of my money back to Erin and the baby. I kept just enough to scrape by, barely covering toiletries, a snack here and there, and maybe a cheap phone card to call home when we hit port. I was rationing dollars and stress. Every dollar I sent back was supposed to keep Erin afloat to help prepare for our daughter's arrival.

My duties on the ship provided my only sense of gravity. I was assigned to the At-Sea Fire Party; a specialized team trained to respond to onboard emergencies, particularly shipboard fires. On a massive carrier like the *Kennedy*, fire is a nightmare scenario. You can't call 911 in the middle of the ocean. *We* were the fire department. We trained relentlessly: donning fire-fighting gear in minutes, sealing hatches, dragging hoses, and learning to contain chemical and electrical fires in pitch-dark compartments. It was intense, gritty work; suffocating, exhausting, essential. I didn't mind the weight of the responsibility. In a way, it gave me purpose. I couldn't be there for Erin, but I could be *useful* here.

And then we hit the Strait of Hormuz.

Anyone who's sailed through it knows the static in the air; it's one of the most dangerous stretches of water in the world. On one side is Oman, on the other, Iran. That stretch of water has been all over the news in recent months here in 2026. That day, something felt off from the start. We were ordered to our stations, suits half-zipped, ready to go. I was in Repair Locker 4-5-Forward; just under the island on the starboard side. No windows, no outside noise: just the hum of the ship and the sound of our own breathing.

Then 1MC, which is the ship's intercom system, crackled to life.

'Missiles inbound.'

The voice was calm, almost matter-of-fact, which made it terrifying. Multiple targets were identified. Inbound. Time to impact: two minutes. My blood turned to ice. We dressed out completely, pulling on the heavy firefighting ensembles and sealing our masks. My heart pounded so loud I couldn't hear the 1MC anymore. Someone cracked a nervous joke, but it died in the air. No one laughed.

I leaned into the cold steel of the bulkhead, bracing for the impact.

I remember thinking: *This is it. I'm never going to meet my daughter.* The thought gutted me; ripped through whatever professional mask I was wearing and exposed a scared, 21-year-old kid underneath. I was fucking scared. I could see the faces of my parents, the daughter I hadn't even met, and Erin, and I felt helpless regret. I was a 21-year-old, and I was prepared to die in a dark passageway without ever having held my child. I joined the Navy fully aware that I may have been called upon to die for my country, but one still hopes that it never comes to that, it doesn't make it easier.

Then, with ten seconds to impact, the call came: 'Stand down.'

It was a surprise drill. A 'stress test' from the command. We slowly unzipped our gear. Nobody spoke. Even one of my co-workers, a guy who claimed to be a die-hard atheist, was quietly whispering prayers when he thought no one was watching.

That night, lying in my rack, I couldn't sleep. The image of my daughter's face; one I hadn't even seen yet; was burned into my mind. I clutched the corner of a worn photograph of Erin and me and stared at the ceiling, thinking about all the things I hadn't said, all the moments I was going to miss. The truth was, I was prepared to die in that passageway. But I wasn't prepared for what that *meant.* I wasn't ready to be just a memory to my child before she even took her first breath.

That moment aged me. It changed the deployment from the job I signed on for into a countdown to getting home.

Our daughter, Kathleen, was born on June 21st while I was still out at sea. I did what I could to stay connected, rationing my expensive conversations like they were oxygen. Each time I hung up, I felt farther away. Eventually, Erin stopped answering. Weeks passed. My letters went unanswered, and I was stuck halfway around the world with no idea what was going on. I was worried; with a million things were going through my mind. I couldn't concentrate on work, and I wasn't eating much of anything. I finally got hold of my mom and asked if she could try calling. It wasn't until my mom finally got through to her that I found out; Erin was filing for divorce. She didn't have the courage to tell me herself, and had my mom not found out, when would she have told me?

I don't think there was anything up until this point in my life that made me angrier. For the first time in my life, I felt a hatred toward another person. I hated myself almost as much. There were moments when I would take the trash out to the port quarter of the ship at the end of the day, staring toward the horizon. I'd watch the trash bags go under the wake of the ship as we sailed into the night, imagining myself as one of them. I could have jumped and ended it: the pain, the hate, all of it.

But Grandma survived much worse, and she never reached that point. Her survival would have been in vain if I jumped. Looking back now, a famous movie line comes to mind: '*It's just a flesh wound.*' It's my way of rationalizing the severity of my problems to the fact that it wasn't the end of the world. It was excruciatingly painful, of course, but it wasn't the end.

I had left for deployment, trusting that everything was solid back home and that we were building something. Instead, I came back to find my marriage gone, my daughter born without me there, and my life in financial ruin. It was the first time something inside of me broke. At the time, Erin and Kathleen were my whole world. I was a father and husband, until it was taken away. I was no longer a husband, and I had never met my daughter yet; I was gutted. I was so angry at one point that I took my wedding band off and threw it out in the middle of the Mediterranean Sea. My ring now a memory of a time passed like my marriage now was.

During deployment, most of my pay had gone back home to Erin and the baby; rent, essentials, baby supplies, doctor visits, whatever they needed. I kept next to nothing for myself. And yet, when I came home, I discovered that the Navy had overpaid me during the cruise, and was now clawing it back. Once again, just like a year and a half prior: my paychecks were gutted. It was a cruel sense of déjà vu; I was making a fraction of my normal checks every two weeks, and I hadn't even finished repaying the overpayments from Connecticut. I had to borrow money from my dad just to keep my car from being repossessed. I was in my early twenties, a new father, and I was completely broke.

Meanwhile, Erin was back in Philly with our daughter,

living with her father. From what I learned later; she had already moved on. Another man, Bob, appeared to be in the picture. I felt like a ghost, like I never existed in their lives. I wanted to go see my daughter, to meet her, to be in her life, but I didn't even have enough money to get to Philadelphia. The thought of hitchhiking crossed my mind. I was a sailor, trained to respond under fire, but I wasn't prepared for this kind of emptiness; financially drained, emotionally hollow.

It wasn't until; over a year later; that I could finally pull together enough money and resolve to make the trip to see my daughter for the first time. I went up to take care of custody papers and finalize the divorce that I had put off for so long.

Baby Kathleen in 1998, first time meeting her.

Looking back, I know I could have fought harder to get Erin to withdraw the divorce, but I always had a mindset, that since those actions entered our marriage, the divorce filing, the thought she didn't want to be with me even though I did nothing, I saw it all as poison. If she didn't want me, then I wasn't going to try and convince her, because now that poison had entered my mind. It isn't who I was at that time in my life.

By then, Erin had her own life, her own rhythm, and I was an outsider looking in. I knew my time in the Navy was nearing its end, and I didn't have the will to reenlist. I let the contract expire. I needed space, needed to get out from under the weight of everything. Maybe I'd rejoin someday.

I just needed to figure out who I was without the uniform, without the family I just lost. That day came sooner than I expected. Nine months after separating from the Navy December of 1999, I found myself walking back into a recruiter's office. I was older, a little more weathered, and ready to take the Navy seriously this time. One month later, I was sent to Pensacola for 'A' School to become an Aviation Electrician. I felt like I was finally getting a second chance, and for the first time in years, I was looking forward to the future.

All in all, my first time in the Navy was absolutely brutal. I fell in love, made stupid and irresponsible decisions, and eventually got my heart broken. I had already been divorced before I was even 23 years old. But I learned some lessons as well, lessons that will serve me for a lifetime. I would eventually remember what Grandma had taught me, to be strong, but it was so much easier said than done. I had no idea how she survived what she did when I had wanted to kill myself at least once. I obviously never followed through, and looking back, that time in my life was as much about learning what *not* to do as it was about figuring out who I was. I made a lot of mistakes; some big, some small; but what I've come to understand is that if you're not stumbling, you're probably not pushing yourself out of your comfort zone. Mistakes became my teacher, and life had a way of turning each misstep into a lesson I couldn't have learned any other way.

Through it all, I realized I had to rely on myself more than I ever expected. Sure, I had friends; guys like Kevin, Ruben, Chris, and, of course, Shun; but when it really came down to it, I felt alone in most of the tough decisions. Shun and I were close, but even he was wired to look out for himself first. That was just who he was. What surprised me most was the strength I didn't know I had. There were plenty of moments when I felt like I was spiraling; going UA, the fallout from my marriage, getting caught up in relationships, numbing myself with alcohol, letting dark and intrusive thoughts enter my consciousness; but I didn't stay down. I started to see situations more clearly, with fewer illusions and more accountability. I learned that reactions matter just as much as the events themselves. Every time life knocked me sideways, I got better at standing back up and choosing a wiser next step. It wasn't graceful, but it was growth. It's what grandma had done her whole life.

When I first joined the Navy, I was a blank slate; just a kid straight out of high school with no real direction or sense of what I wanted out of life. I didn't carry dreams of grandeur or specific goals. I just knew I needed something different, something bigger than the life I had known. The Navy wasn't just a job or a stepping stone; it was the crucible that would shape me into who I was becoming. It didn't change me overnight, but it gave me the space, and sometimes the hard lessons, to grow into a man. Over the course of four deployments and through countless nights alone at sea, I was given time to reflect.

I thought deeply about who I was, who I wanted to become, and how every decision, even the misguided ones, had something to teach me. That kind of reflection is both a blessing and a burden. With the freedom to shape my own path came the crushing weight of responsibility. I didn't always make the right choices. In fact, I made plenty of the wrong ones. But those missteps were necessary. Without them, I wouldn't have learned to navigate life with the clarity and purpose I eventually gained.

Through every duty station, every deployment, every hardship; I learned. I learned that mistakes are part of progress. I learned that relying on yourself doesn't mean being alone; it means being accountable.

While I had friends along the way, Shun was the only one I could ever halfway lean on, he was the one constant I had from the beginning, not to be confused with consistent, because he was not that at all. At the end of the day, it was on me to pick myself up, to keep pushing forward, to figure out how to live with the choices I made and use them to become better. The Navy taught me discipline, flexibility, and self-reliance; but more than that, it taught me how to become a decent human being, not just through success but through failure. I had to learn to let go of control, to stop forcing things to happen, and instead let life unfold; even when that meant enduring painful consequences because that's how growth happens: not in perfection, but in persistence.

Chapter 9
The Tour Continues

Back then, anyone that was enlisted in the Navy, you eventually expected to be deployed to multiple places, with each deployment lasting for a maximum of 6 months, *much different* from today's operational tempo. It's hard to explain to people back home what it really means to step foot into a different country, not as a tourist, but as a service member, eyes open, watching, learning. We were sent to multiple places as part of our deployments and never really stayed in one place long enough to learn much or get comfortable.

My first deployment on the JFK wasn't just my first real Navy visit overseas; it was the first time I had truly seen the world beyond the edges of everything I had known. It was my first time being so far from home, so far from everything familiar. And I was still young and impressionable, trying to make sense of life, duty, identity, and the world around me; all at the same time.

When you grow up in one country, especially one like America, it's easy to believe the way you live is *the* standard. But when you step outside that bubble and really start to walk the streets of places so different from your own, it does something to you. It cracks something open. And for me, it created a deeper, unexpected empathy. The kind of understanding that doesn't come from reading a book or watching a documentary. It only comes when you've seen people's lives up close, not just from a hotel window or guided bus tour.

It wasn't like the movies or travel guides, and it sure wasn't anything like life back in America. That's not to say it was all bad, just different. Simpler in some ways and harder in others. You'd see kids playing soccer in dusty alleyways, women washing clothes in a river while laughing like they didn't have a care in the world, and men selling handmade goods on streets where the buildings looked like they had seen more history than we could ever learn in a textbook.

These weren't just quick photo ops for someone's scrapbook. They were real moments that made you stop and think. You start realizing how much we take for granted in the States: Basic utilities, fresh food, and a sense of safety. Over there, survival was sometimes the name of the game, and that sense of daily struggle was carved into the faces of those we passed. Still, even in places that looked broken, there was a strange kind of beauty. The kind that made you reevaluate your own life and ask questions you weren't always ready to answer.

Seeing how people made the most of what they had left a mark on me. It made me reflect on how Grandma made the most of where she was in life at different stages. It made me realize how insulated and oblivious we can be in the U.S., not out of arrogance but lack of experience.

In many of the cities we visited, daily life was tough, but it carried on with a strength I still admire. And those images, the children laughing barefoot in the mud, the crowded markets brimming with life, the quiet toughness in people's eyes, those things stay with you.

That contrast between what we know and what we witness abroad teaches us humility. It reminds us that no matter how tough we think we've had it, someone out there is waking up every day and fighting just to make it to the next. I wouldn't trade those experiences for anything. I was 21 at the time and would never have expected to learn what I did on tour to be taught in any high school or college. These experiences taught me more about life than I ever could have learned sitting at a desk or inside a cubicle.

To put a cherry on top of my learning, I didn't usually do the touristy things, not because I wasn't curious, but because money was always tight, and those tours added up quickly. So, I made my own experiences. I would walk for hours, getting lost on purpose in old neighborhoods, back alleys, and street markets, especially in places like Greece or Dubai. While most others were sipping drinks on guided sightseeing excursions, I was out exploring the real city behind the postcard gloss. Meeting citizens living there. Experiencing their lives and not the one curated for a visitor.

I remember wandering through small streets in Rhodes or Corfu, where the cobblestone streets were older than the country I came from. I'd pass crumbling doorways, laundry lines strung between balconies, and shopkeepers who barely spoke English but smiled anyway. In Dubai, I walked through the Gold Souk and other local markets, with vendors yelling over each other in Arabic and spices hanging in the air like smoke. It was overwhelming in the best way: Chaotic, colorful, and absolutely alive.

My meals? Usually from street carts and food trucks, back before "food truck culture" became trendy. It was different back then. Less curated, more authentic. Shawarma from a rusted cart, kebabs grilled right in front of me on the side of the road, and fresh bread handed to me with a nod instead of a smile. These weren't meals for social media; they were for survival, and they tasted like the country itself.

And even though I was learning and experiencing so much, this wasn't some romantic, globe-trotting adventure. I carried a lot with me: heartache, depression, and anger. All those things followed me across borders and time zones. But I also found something else out there in the in-between: internal growth. Quiet, meaningful growth. The kind that creeps up on you when you're far from everything and everyone you know, with nothing but your own thoughts echoing back.

I didn't come back from that deployment, the same kid who left. I had seen more. Felt more. And most of all, I learned that the world is far more complicated, more painful, and more beautiful than I ever could have imagined. And that knowledge, earned through soles worn down by foreign pavement and meals eaten standing on street corners, stayed with me.

Our deployment was what we in the Navy called a Med Cruise, short for Mediterranean Cruise, though I can tell you right now that it was nothing like the cruises civilians take for fun. There were no pool decks or fruity drinks with umbrellas, no buffets or relaxing days at sea. This was the Navy's version of a cruise, which meant long hours, watch rotations, constant maintenance, and the occasional port call that reminded you the world was metaphorically a whole lot bigger than just the ocean you were floating on.

We crossed the Atlantic Ocean, eventually slicing through the Strait of Gibraltar, that narrow gateway where Europe and Africa almost shake hands. On the other side of that passage, we entered the Mediterranean, and that's where the real journey began.

Our first stop was in Marseille, France. There's something surreal about pulling into a place that's older than your country, knowing you're walking streets that have stood for centuries. After that, the order gets a little fuzzy. We didn't follow a neat itinerary like a tour guide's brochure, but I can still see the names and places burned into my memory.

We made port in several cities across Spain; Palma, Benidorm, Valencia, and Tarragona. Each had its own personality. Palma had that laid-back island feel, the kind of place where you could lose track of time watching waves roll into the harbor. Benidorm was more like a beach town with energy, tourists, nightlife, and the kind of coastal atmosphere that made it hard to believe you were still on a military deployment. Valencia and Tarragona had their own flavors, too. Historic, colorful, and rich with local culture.

From Spain, we moved on to Koper, Slovenia. It was a quieter, less tourist-driven port that still carried the charm of old Europe. Then there was Cannes, France, where the luxury and elegance were obvious the moment you stepped off the ship. You could feel the history and smell the money in the air like it was baked into the buildings and cobblestone streets.

We continued east, pulling into Corfu and Rhodes in Greece, each one like stepping into a postcard. Ancient architecture standing guard over turquoise water and little cafés with food that reminded you there was more to life than the galley chow back on the ship.

One of the more memorable stops was Haifa, Israel. There was a quiet intensity to that place. You could sense the depth of the region's history, spiritual, cultural, and political, all pressing in around you. I still remember sitting on a barge that pulled up alongside the JFK where we were anchored out in the Bay of Haifa.

The barge was there to offload our sewage waste. My job

as an HT was to sit there on watch making sure pumping operations were done and ran smoothly as scheduled. There was a local that sat there with me when I was on watch for 8 hours. We talked about what life was like in our respective countries, while he had this little kettle and a heat source making us some fresh ground Turkish coffee. It was dark and grainy, but so good. Those few moments are some of the most vivid memories from any deployment I was on. It wasn't just sightseeing. It was standing on ground that had seen thousands of years of conflict and faith, and trying to process what that meant in the short time you were allowed ashore.

Eventually, we transited through the Suez Canal, moving into a different chapter and main focus of any deployment. That narrow strip of water, cutting through Egypt, took us from the calm blues of the Mediterranean into the hotter, dustier waters of the Middle East. On the other side, our mission changed, the pace picked up, and we spent the next few months adjusting to new objectives and new threats.

During that part of the deployment, we pulled into Bahrain, a small island country in the Persian Gulf. During my deployment on the ship, I was assigned to the shop that handled any maintenance or other issues regarding the plumbing throughout the ship, so I had some time on my hands that I used to spend outside, and the hustle and bustle of Bahrain really caught my eye. It had its own kind of energy. American fast-food chains are wedged between ancient marketplaces, sand, and sea, colliding with modern development. We were a long way from home, and it showed.

Looking back, it's hard to wrap my head around all the places we saw on that one deployment. It wasn't just a Med Cruise; it was an eye-opener. A lesson in perspective. A reminder that the world is full of people living lives we rarely think about, in places we'll never fully understand, all carrying stories just as real and intricate as our own. Of course, today, in a new age of technology, anyone can get a glimpse of the world.

From how I describe it, deployment and going on tour might sound like a paradise for travelers, jumping from place to place, most expenses paid, getting paid to do it, and experiencing the joys of travel without the financial dread that is attached to it, but it wasn't sunshine and rainbows. The price I paid was higher than most things.

At that point in my life, everything still felt like it was in its early stages, like I was barely getting started. I was just stepping into fatherhood, something I had genuinely looked forward to, and for the first time, I felt like I had something deeply meaningful to live for. I was proud, hopeful, even happy. But those feelings didn't last long. Very quickly, things spun into turmoil, and what should have been a joyful season of growth became a time of heartbreak and isolation.

It was like the floor had dropped out from beneath me. Suddenly, I found myself in a world where it felt like everyone had moved on without me. I was across the ocean on my first real deployment, and yet my thoughts were constantly back home, wondering if my daughter was okay, if anyone even thought about me, if I still mattered. I wasn't given much say in how everything played out, and that lack of control, of agency, sat heavily on my shoulders. It was like watching your own life unfold from behind a locked window, unable to reach out or participate in it.

That disconnect mirrored how it felt to be on deployment in general. You leave. You go do your job, follow orders, and play your part in the bigger machine. And when it's over, you come back to a world that kept turning without you. It wasn't just about missing big things; it was all the small stuff, too. You'd hear about new movies that came out while you were gone, Men in Black, Austin Powers, and realize you were months behind on even the most basic cultural moments. It was a reminder that you weren't there, not for any of it.

There was one moment in particular that burned itself into my memory. We were in Greece, walking around on liberty, just trying to soak in the experience. I wandered into a music store, the kind of place I always liked to kill time in. As I was flipping through CDs, I heard a song playing overhead, Puff Daddy's "I'll Be Missing You." At first, I thought it was The Police's "Every Breath You Take," but there was something different in it. The tone, the message, the pain; it hit differently. And in that moment, it landed on me hard how the world back home was still spinning, creating new art, new memories, new stories; without me in it.

I had never been away long enough to feel truly left behind. That day in the music store, it all became real. The distance wasn't just measured in miles; it was measured in experiences I would never get back. That song wasn't just on the radio; it became a soundtrack to my disconnection.

Even though I was technically experiencing something incredible, my first time traveling outside of the United States, it was hard to enjoy it the way I should have. It was a landmark moment in my life, something many people never get to do. But instead of wonder and awe, I felt torn, disconnected, captive to a life I couldn't reach back home. And the worst part? I didn't even know if my newborn daughter was okay.

The beauty of the Mediterranean, the history, the culture, it was all there. But my heart wasn't. It was thousands of miles away, wondering if I was being remembered at all.

One of the biggest challenges during that deployment, and really for anyone serving back then, was the sheer difficulty of communicating with loved ones. These were the days before everyone had smartphones in their pockets, before Wi-Fi was expected in every corner of the globe. Staying connected wasn't just difficult; it felt almost impossible at times.

Our options were limited. If we wanted to hear someone's voice back home, we had to rely on expensive international phone cards. They were spotty at best and often unreliable, not justifying how expensive they really were and how I often got debt collection letters for not paying my MCI or whatever phone card bills I had. You'd find a payphone, spend half your time trying to dial through confusing menus, only to get disconnected midway through the call or hear so much static it hardly felt worth it. And even when the call went through, the cost meant you had to keep it short. You learned quickly that even a five-minute conversation was a luxury you couldn't afford often, hence the expensive phone card bills.

So, more often than not, we turned to good old-fashioned letters, snail mail, written by hand, folded into envelopes, and shipped off across oceans and time zones. But even that wasn't as simple as it sounds. A letter could take weeks to arrive, and depending on where the ship was, it could be even longer. Worse, they would show up completely out of order. You'd open a letter and find yourself confused. There'd be references to things you hadn't read about yet and emotional responses to questions you hadn't even seen.

To fix that, it became a smart habit, almost a rule, to write a number at the top of every letter so you could try to read them in the right order. Letter 3 wouldn't make much sense if you hadn't gotten Letter 2 yet, and by the time you got to Letter 5, you might've already misunderstood what Letter 1 was really about. That's just how it went. Trying to keep a relationship steady with weeks-long gaps between exchanges, mixed-up timelines, and nothing but hope to fill in the blanks.

On top of that, there was the financial juggling act, which added a whole other layer of stress. Erin and I shared a single bank account, and managing that from opposite ends of the world was a mess. I'd pull money out from an ATM in some foreign port city, where the receipt was printed in local currency, so I had no clear idea how much I'd actually spent in U.S. dollars. Meanwhile, she'd be back home spending what she needed on her end, and we had no real way to communicate in real-time about it.

It wasn't like today, where you can just open an app and check your balance or send a quick text to coordinate expenses. Yeah, you could get balances back then, but it wasn't as close to instant as it is today. It was almost like multiple checks you forgot was out there, spending money you didn't actually have, all hitting your account at one time. You had to be good at balancing your account. Back then, everything was a guessing game. You didn't know what had cleared, what hadn't, or if you were about to overdraft. And every time that happened, it wasn't just about the money; it became an argument waiting to happen, with stress piling on top of already stretched emotions, all because the tools simply didn't exist to make it easier.

That combination of uncertain communication and financial stress could wear on you fast. It made an already demanding deployment feel even more disconnected. And it reminded you just how far from home you really were. Not just physically, but emotionally too.

Chapter 10
The End of the Beginning

My first deployment, filled with interesting developments and grueling days, finally ended after 6 months in November 1997. Even though I always knew that I'd eventually go back, it felt pretty exciting to officially start that transit back home.

Deployments before September 11, 2001, had a rhythm to them, a routine and predictability that let you mentally map out your year. You knew when you were leaving and when you were coming back. There was a rotation, that predictability, in a strange way, offered a sense of comfort.

However, even though I was excited about finally coming back to the States, I carried a heavy mix of emotions with me. There was anxiety. There was anger. There was sadness. It was a messy bundle of feelings, knowing that what I was walking back into was a life unraveling. My marriage was crumbling, and I knew a divorce was coming. I had watched my parents go through one, and I had sworn I'd never put my own kids through that. But life has a way of forcing your hand.

Part of me just wanted to vanish. I thought about staying in Spain, Italy, or anywhere else we had visited. I'd daydream about walking off base and starting over in some old cobblestone town by the sea. I wasn't ready to face the wreckage waiting for me at home. Reality, especially the kind you can't avoid, has a way of sucking the life out of you. Coming back after a deployment should have been a relief. But instead of celebration, I felt dread. It was as if I were walking into a movie that had kept playing without me, and I had no idea what had happened since I was gone.

When we finally returned, family, friends, and acquaintances, as always, wondered how it felt coming back or how exciting it must have been visiting exotic lands. Normally that would be the fun part. My seniors in the Navy were with me the whole time, mentoring and supporting me in ways that only those in the trenches alongside you can. They knew what I had been through because, for the most part, they were going through the same things. But my parents, my friends, and everyone else back home didn't know the full picture.

They'd ask a few things here and there, mostly about the places I saw, thinking it was cool that I had the chance to travel. And sure, I shared a story or two, but it was different this time. I didn't have a bunch of tales or funny experiences to unload because most of that deployment was tainted by the stress, the lack of money, and, most of all, by the divorce looming over everything. It dulled everything I had experienced. I felt like I had gone somewhere remarkable and returned as a different version of myself, one I wasn't quite sure how to explain to anyone else.

Even though there were many negative feelings bottled up

within me, regret was not one of them. I didn't feel an ounce of regret about joining the Navy or getting deployed. In fact, I was incredibly proud.

Knowing that I was part of something bigger than myself was one of the only things that truly kept me grounded. Wearing the uniform, serving aboard a United States Navy vessel, and committing myself to a cause greater than any one person gave me a sense of purpose I had never known before. It was like an anchor in the middle of a storm that threatened to rip everything else away.

I served on the USS John F. Kennedy during that deployment, and that alone carried weight. There was a history to that ship, a legacy that meant something to those of us fortunate enough to be assigned to it. What added even more meaning was a quote I came across from President John F. Kennedy himself. He once said, *"Any man who may be asked in this century what he did to make his life worthwhile, I think can respond with a good deal of pride and satisfaction: 'I served in the United States Navy.'"*

That quote struck a chord in me that has never stopped ringing. It put words to what I was feeling at a time when so much else in my life felt out of control. And it gave me something to hold onto, not just in that moment but in the years that followed. That quote, that idea, would stay with me and quietly guide the decisions that led to my twenty-year career in the Navy.

Getting my first chevron as a Third-Class Petty Officer in 1998 on the USS John F Kennedy (first row, 2nd from the left).

In many ways, my pride in serving became the thread that stitched me together when everything else felt like it was unraveling. It reminded me that no matter what pain I was carrying, no matter what chaos I had to return to, I had done something worthwhile, and that meant something.

Other than bolstering my pride, my time away in the Navy also gave me many life lessons. However, if I had to pinpoint the most important thing I learned during my time away, it would be the realization that our country really is something unique, or at least, it used to be. It was a country that performed miracles, miracles like the rescue of my grandma from the Japanese.

Back then, stepping off the ship into other parts of the world, you could feel the difference almost immediately. It felt like we were living in a society that was light-years ahead in so many ways. Technology, opportunity, infrastructure, and freedom. Those things were not just buzzwords in a recruiting pamphlet. They were real, and they were easy to take for granted when you had never experienced anything else.

Of course, that perspective has shifted with time. A lot of what we believed was due to the fact that we simply saw and heard less. The world felt smaller back then, or maybe just less loud. The twenty-four-hour news cycles, the endless commentary, the constant negativity, and division did not hit you every second of the day like it does now. In some ways, being less aware of all the noise gave us room to focus on the good and to carry pride without cynicism. And honestly, I do not think that was such a bad thing.

Even so, this deployment taught me more than just national pride. It pushed me to become more open-minded, more accepting, and more curious about the world around me. That was never something I struggled with too much before. I was always someone who tried to understand people, but traveling like that, seeing how others lived, what they valued, and what they struggled with, deepened that part of me. It made me want to know more, to connect more.

What I began to crave, more than anything, was culture. Not the packaged version you get in museums or on travel shows, but the kind that surrounds you when you walk down a market street in a foreign city or sit in a local café where you are the only outsider. After deployment, that craving did not go away. If anything, it grew stronger.

However, as proud as I was of what I had accomplished so far, I would be lying if I said I did not seriously think about getting out of the Navy at that point. The thought crept in more than once. Despite the pride I felt wearing the uniform and being part of something bigger than myself, there was still a part of me that carried a heavy sense of frustration and emotional fatigue. It had been a rough few years, personally, mentally, and emotionally, and it was hard not to link that back to the life I was living in uniform.

There were moments when I felt like the Navy had taken more from me than it had given. The strain on relationships, the time away from family, and the challenges I faced both at sea and back home all added up, and it was tempting to place the blame squarely on the Navy itself. But when I really took a step back and looked at it honestly, I had to admit that it was not all the Navy's fault. A lot of it was me. My choices, my mindset, and how I handled things. I was young and still learning how to navigate everything that came with being a Sailor, a husband, and eventually, a father. There were lessons I had not yet learned, and that realization was humbling.

At the same time, there were practical reasons I started considering an exit, too. I thought about what it might be like to return to civilian life, to reset and maybe find a different path. But I also knew that if I was going to stay or leave, it had to be for the right reasons. Not because I was angry or worn out, but because I had taken the time to really reflect on what mattered.

In that reflection, I found clarity, and that is what ultimately helped me decide to keep going.

One thing was certain, anywhere I was able to settle with a support system in place already, I knew culture and diversity would be scarce. Those things were not present anywhere near where I grew up. I knew I would miss the feeling of being surrounded by stories and people who see the world through a different lens.

Chapter 11
Exiting the Navy

After about a year and a half of working on the JFK, I decided it was time to make my exit. It wasn't that long, but with my marriage and everything going on, I determined that it might be time for me to step back and focus on myself for a bit.

Although I carried a deep sense of pride for having served, I could not help but feel that the Navy had been the reason, or at least what I believed at the time, for the difficult years I faced early on in my service. In moments of quiet reflection, however, I came to realize that it was not truly the Navy that had caused those struggles. The weight of those challenges, I understood at last, rested on my own shoulders. I had made choices that shaped my path, and it was on me to step back, take stock of where I stood, and consider how best to move forward. I was accountable for my actions.

That realization brought a certain clarity, and with it, the decision to separate from the Navy became easier to accept. The truth was that advancement opportunities were limited in the job I held at the time. I was working as a welder and pipefitter, and while I valued the work and gave it my all, the prospects for rising through the ranks were slim. The advancement quotas in my field were poor, and that reality weighed heavily on my mind. I saw it firsthand in the lives of those around me. I knew fellow Sailors, good men who were SMEs in our work, had served honorably and built solid reputations, who were retiring at the rank of E-5. These were individuals who had done everything right. They were respected by their peers and seniors alike, but the system simply did not allow them to rise any further. The opportunities just were not there, no matter how deserving they might have been.

I had only recently been promoted to E-4 in the year before I chose to leave, and as I looked ahead, the idea of spending another 15 years in service with perhaps only one more promotion to hope for seemed unbearable. The thought of being locked into that kind of slow progression, despite hard work and dedication, felt stifling. It was not the future I wanted for myself. My hope was that with time and distance, I could find a new approach. One that would allow me to return in a capacity that offered greater room for growth and a better chance at building the kind of career I had envisioned when I first joined.

There was no singular event or defining moment that prompted my decision to leave, it was a growing desire to pause, reflect, and seek out a path that would offer greater opportunities for professional advancement.

What made this choice even more necessary was the resistance I encountered from within the Navy itself. Despite my determination to cross over into another job field, one where I believed I could truly thrive, I was met with refusal. The Navy had its own reasons, of course. Having recently achieved the rank of E-4, I was informed that a transition to a different field would not be possible, at least not for a long time. That reality left me feeling trapped, as if the door to further growth had been firmly shut for now. And so, I chose to take control of my own future. I stepped away, not in bitterness or regret, but with the hope that by doing so, I could forge a path that would offer the kind of progress and fulfillment I had been seeking all along.

The final decision was made towards the end of 1998 to make an exit in April of 1999 with terminal leave. As my time in the Navy was drawing to a close, I found myself reflecting on the connections I had made along the way. Truth be told, I was never someone who had a wide circle of close friends, but I did have a small group of people who genuinely cared. They let me know that I would be missed, and together, we made sure to make the most of the time we had left before my departure. We spent many nights out, determined to enjoy ourselves and create memories that would last.

Several evenings each week, we would find ourselves at the clubs scattered across Jacksonville.

Of all these places, Masquerade and Crazy Horse stood out as my personal favorites. On one side, Masquerade, pulsed with pop, hip-hop, dance music, while the other, Crazy Horse, provided the vibe of a lively country bar. I always found myself having the best time there, as if the mix of themes gave everyone something to enjoy. It was also those times when I let my pain get the better of me, drinking way too much.

When we wanted a change of pace, we would head out toward the beach. There was a place called Harmonious Monks that became a regular stop for us. During the day, it served as a restaurant, but at night, it transformed into a bar that came alive with live music. The night would always end the same way: A cover of Don McLean's "American Pie" would fill the air, and the crowd would respond with wild enthusiasm. It was not unusual to see people dancing up on the bar or standing on the tabletops, swept up in the moment. Every outing felt like a mission where the goal was to have as much fun as possible and, if luck was on my side, maybe meet a girl who would be interested enough to invite me back to her place.

For those nights when all we were after was cheap beer and good food, we would go to Buckets Bar and Grill. They served the best wings in town, and what truly made the place memorable was their beer night. They offered a deal where you could fill any container you brought in with draft beer for an amount so cheap it was almost laughable. I do not remember the exact price anymore, whether it was a quarter or something close to it, but it was certainly low enough that no one ever complained.

As for my decision to leave, I was not pressured or

pushed. My Division Chiefs did make an effort to get me to reconsider. They offered me what would have been a comfortable role in the carpenter shop within my division. It was a one-man shop tasked with maintaining the wooden handrails that lined parts of the ship. The job also involved crafting wooden keepsakes shaped like the flight deck of the Kennedy, which were given to recognize people who were transferring or separating. These keepsakes were carefully made, with inlays and a glossy, clear coat. I had done some training in the shop earlier in my career, so it was not unfamiliar work. I still have the one that was made for me when I got out. It is a reminder of that chapter of my life.

Even though they made the offer, I knew that their support for my decision was genuine. In truth, energy was not usually spent trying to change the mind of someone who had already decided to go unless that person had stood out in some exceptional way. I was not one of those Sailors. I was just an average member of the crew, doing my job without drawing too much attention. And so, they wished me well as I prepared to move on.

Not just my friends, but I was also a bit sad about leaving. The Navy had been more than just a job; it had been my world, a place that made me who I was in ways I was only beginning to understand. As much as I had prepared myself for this decision, part of me could not help but feel the weight of what I was walking away from. The camaraderie, the structure, the sense of belonging that came with wearing the uniform - all of it was about to become part of my past.

There were moments when I came close to second-guessing what I had chosen to do. It is never easy to step away from something that has defined so much of who you are. But by then, the point of no return had come and gone. The documents had been signed, and the paperwork was completed. The decision had been set in motion, and there was no turning back. Despite the doubts that crept in during quiet moments, I reminded myself of the reasons why I had made this choice. I held onto those reasons to steady myself.

For the most part, I felt confident. I believed I was doing what I needed to do for my future. But I would be lying if I said there was no nervousness. I knew the road ahead would not be easy. The plan was to move back in with my mom and Curt in Nevada, at least for a while, until I could get back on my feet and figure out my next steps. The thought of starting over was daunting, but I told myself that sometimes, in order to move forward, you have to be willing to take a step back first.

At that point in my life, my family situation was steady and supportive, something I was deeply grateful for as I prepared to transition out of the Navy and start over. My mom and Curt were living in Elko at the time, and our relationship remained close. Despite everything that was shifting around me, I could count on them. They stood firmly by my side, offering encouragement and whatever help I needed as I tried to find my footing again.

When I left the Navy, I moved in with them. They had settled in Spring Creek, a quiet place just beyond a small range of hills that separated it from Elko. Those hills felt like more than just a geographical divide. They marked the distance between my old life and the new one I was trying to build.

I quickly found myself in search of steady work. I needed to find something to help me regain my footing while I figured out what the future would hold. Before long, I was able to secure a job as a security guard at a local mine, Newmont Gold Mining. The site was located several miles West of Elko, out in the vast, open stretches of the Nevada high desert.

There was a quietness to it at times, surrounded by that wide expanse of land, and my patrols gave me space to think as I adjusted to civilian life.

Not long after I moved in, things began to change for them as well. Before the end of 1999, Mom's work brought about another move. Her job offered her a transfer, and so she and Curt packed up and relocated to Lakeland, Florida. I went with them, knowing it was the right choice at the time. Roy would follow not long after, joining us down in Florida, and it gave me comfort to have him close again. Even though life had taken us all on different paths, we found our way back to one another, and that sense of family kept me grounded through it all.

As for my first marriage, Erin and I had reached the end of our road together. The divorce became final in August of 1998, just before I separated from the Navy. It was a difficult chapter to close, but by then, we both understood it was what needed to happen. There was a finality to it that brought sadness, of course, but also a sense of resolution. It marked the end of one part of my life and the beginning of another, a chance to start fresh with the lessons I had gathered along the way.

When my family moved to Lakeland, Florida, I took whatever work I could find just to bring in a paycheck while we searched for a place to settle. Once we found a place, I landed a position at Service Merchandise, working alongside Roy. That job brought with it a little more enjoyment. For anyone who remembers, Service Merchandise was known for the catalogs they sent out every Christmas, the ones kids would flip through for hours, circling toys and gadgets they hoped to find under the tree. It reminded me a lot of Sears back in those days. My role was in the warehouse, where I loaded customers' purchases into their cars, making sure everything they bought was ready for them to take home.

At the same time, I also worked at a Walmart Distribution Center in Winter Haven. I found the pacing of civilian jobs to be very different from what I had grown used to in the Navy.

The change was immediate and noticeable, and it touched nearly every part of my routine. During my time in service, there was a certain security that came with the uniform. In the Navy, it was incredibly difficult to lose your position. Getting fired was not something most had to worry about unless a person made choices that crossed serious lines, such as getting caught using drugs or acting violently. Even then, I had seen cases where people stayed on despite their missteps. That sense of stability, for better or worse, had always been part of life in uniform.

Stepping into the civilian workforce, I found myself in an entirely different world. For the first time, I was working jobs where I had to clock in and out, where being on time and staying sharp were crucial in ways that felt new to me. There was no longer that built-in safety net of military structure to fall back on. It was an adjustment, but one I accepted because I knew this was simply part of the next stage of my life.

Mentally, it did not weigh heavily on me. I reminded myself often that this was temporary. The jobs I worked, three of them altogether between Nevada and Florida, were all part of a transitional period, a necessary step as I figured out where I was headed next. All told, that stretch lasted less than six months, a relatively short chapter as I moved from the world I had known in the Navy to the one I was building on my own. Through it all, I kept my focus on the bigger picture, knowing that what lay ahead would eventually offer more stability and support. Maybe it was time for a return to something old?

Chapter 12
The Crucible

Even after I stepped away that first time, I always knew deep down that I would return to the Navy. That intention was never far from my mind. I had simply needed space to collect myself, regroup, and figure out where I wanted to go from there. The companionship I had experienced during my first tour stayed with me like a memory that wouldn't fade. I missed it; the shared moments, the laughter that came in between the chaos, the sense of belonging that was hard to find anywhere else.

However, if I were going to go back, it had to be with a purpose. While my intentions when I first joined were good, they were slightly misguided and naïve. I had to make sure that the path I chose this time would offer better opportunities for growth and advancement. That was the goal from the beginning: to find a career track that would actually take me somewhere. More than anything, I was thinking about my daughter. I knew the only real way I could be financially strong enough to be part of her life was to find stability, and that wasn't going to happen unless I made a significant move. I had to do this for myself. I had to build something better. Rejoining was always part of the design. And looking back now, I see it clearly for what it was: the first real move that would carry me toward the life I was meant to build.

But in June 2000, while I was at 'A' school at NAS Pensacola, everything came to a violent halt.

***

Roy Alma Thornock. R.A.T. I never let him live those initials down. He also hated his middle name growing up; he thought it sounded like a girl's name, even though it was passed down through the family on my dad's side. Born September 21st, 1978, Roy was very good-natured, and even though we fought a lot and couldn't stand when the other was even breathing in our personal space, I knew that when it came down to it, I could count on him to defend me, just like he knew I would be there for him as well.

Roy and I were in the truck after we left the lake, I think.

He was a bright star, a talkative guy. I recall that he was almost held back in kindergarten because he couldn't stop talking. Friends and family referred to him as Roy Boy sometimes. Roy was still living in Lakeland at the time, staying with Mom and Curt right there in the same house where I had been living just before I rejoined the Navy. He had landed a job at the Publix Grocery Distribution Center, pulling the second shift, which meant that he usually clocked out around midnight, heading home late into the quiet hours. There was one particular night, his friend needed a ride, and since Roy had work anyway, he let him borrow his car, a Mercury Sable.

From what we were able to piece together from the police report, Roy's friend had been drinking a lot before he got behind the wheel to come get him. I honestly don't think Roy knew that because if he had, there's no way he would have let the guy drive. They never made it. As they came off the exit ramp from Interstate 4 onto the highway near the house, something went wrong. Terribly wrong. The car flipped, and so did my entire world. Just like that, it was over; both were killed instantly in the wreck.

I've thought a lot about that night. As awful as it sounds, I've always felt that it was probably for the best that the other guy didn't survive. Because if he had lived, I don't know what I would've done. The anger, the pain; I'm not sure I would've had the strength to stop myself from doing something I'd regret for the rest of my life. Maybe I would have done nothing, but I will never know. My entire world shifted in that moment, and the direction my life could have gone from there scares me to this day. That darkness that had bubbled up in the previous phase of my life was churning into a rolling boil, but I didn't know it yet.

***

While all of this was happening, I was at the 'A' school at NAS Pensacola, completing my education to become an Aviation Electrician for the Navy, completely oblivious to the fact that I had just lost my best friend, my brother. It was June 9th, 2000, a Friday I'll never forget. Every day started the same: morning PT followed by classroom instruction, rinse and repeat. That day was supposed to be no different. It was around 07:30, just after PT, and I had gotten to the schoolhouse early, going through my usual routine, prepping before class started. I was the class leader, so I made a point to stay squared away.

Out of nowhere, the Master Chief; who oversaw the entire schoolhouse; came to the classroom I was sitting in while I waited for my classmates to arrive. He asked for me to come to his office. I remember walking down the hallway with a thousand questions racing through my head. Was I in trouble? Had someone complained? Was there some kind of issue with my leadership? I didn't know what to expect, but I sure wasn't ready for what was waiting for me.

The first sign that something was off came when he told me to sit down. That alone stopped me cold. We were normally required to be standing at attention, at ease, or parade rest. We were never told to sit in a setting like that, especially not when getting spoken to by someone so senior. That simple gesture told me this wasn't a standard conversation. He looked at me, really seriously, and asked if I had a brother. I nodded, trying to figure out where this was headed. Then he asked what my brother's name was.

"Roy," I said, my voice barely holding steady.

And then came the blow that would knock the air from my lungs for the rest of my life: he told me he had just received word from the Red Cross. Roy had been killed. An accident. No details yet, just that he was gone. Everything stopped at that moment. The room, the noise from the hallway, the weight of the uniform on my back; all of it just disappeared into silence. I walked out of that office, a different man from the one who walked in. And the life I returned to wasn't the same one I had left behind.

***

The days that followed Roy's death felt like a blur; like I was moving through a world I no longer recognized. I was in absolute disbelief. It felt like the ground beneath me had collapsed, and there was no bottom to land on. I couldn't cry; not at first, not for months. I think part of me shut down completely, like some kind of emotional autopilot kicked in. I didn't allow myself to break down because I felt like I couldn't. Mom had just lost her son, her baby boy, and I thought I needed to be strong for her, to carry the weight and keep it together, like I'd always tried to do. That was my role. So, I stuffed the grief down deep inside, wore a mask of composure, and told myself this is what being strong looks like. But inside, I was drowning.

When I returned to school after the funeral, it felt like I was stepping back into a world that had kept moving without me, the same but different from returning from deployment. I chose to use school as a distraction. I threw myself into the training, into the structure, the schedule; the familiarity of it. Compared to the unpredictability of civilian life, the Navy offered a rhythm, a sense of order that I had missed. In the civilian world, everything felt loosely held together. But in the Navy, the lines were clear. You knew what was expected of you, where you needed to be, and what you had to do. That kind of structure brought a sense of peace I had not even realized I was craving.

I started thinking about my grandma. About my mom. About the tragedies they had endured in their lives and how, despite everything, they never folded. I realized that if I gave up, I'd be dishonoring everything they fought for, it would be all for naught. So, I made a decision. I'd toe the line, and I'd honor them by following the standard they set. When I finally graduated from training, it was more than just another milestone. It felt like a tribute. A way to honor my brother and everyone else who'd made me who I was. I would transfer to my first duty station in the aviation side of the Navy, the HS-3 Tridents out of NAS Jacksonville. Coincidentally, this was the same helicopter squadron that was deployed with me on the Kennedy, my last command for another chapter of my Navy career.

In September, just before his birthday, as soon as I could, I went out and got a tattoo; something permanent, something symbolic. A dragon, fierce and protective, was etched into my skin. And underneath it, protected by the dragon, a banner with Roy's name, and the years he was born and died. It wasn't just ink. It was a memory. It was grief. It was love.

The tattoo I got is to remember my brother after he died.

***

Once again, after reporting to a new command, it was time for deployment, and although I didn't know it at that time, that deployment, the one that began in the shadow of September 11th, would become the most pivotal moment of my entire military career.

I remember standing in our Avionics shop on the 03-Level on the port side of the ship. It had fast access to the flight deck for when we were needed. At that time, I was serving as a flight deck troubleshooter, assigned specifically to the helicopters in our squadron. The job was hands-on, intense, and demanded constant awareness. It was 5:00 p.m., give or take a few minutes, and my shift was preparing to come into work. Some of us were either getting ready to go down to the galley and eat, while a few had just gotten back. We had a T.V. in the shop with the news on.

It was noisy, with about 10 or more of us in there at the same time, we were all abuzz about seeing Flight 11 hit the North Tower. We all thought how bad an *accident* it was, when suddenly it got quiet. We just watched as Flight 175 hit the South Tower. We watched in disgust and horror as the news coverage continued on. As soon as we saw the Pentagon get hit by Flight 77, we felt the ship do a hard turn to port. We were actually on our way leaving the Persian Gulf, had been for about a day I think, and now we had to turn back to defend our country.

Then came October 7th, 2001. While working on my shift, our ship was beginning Operation Enduring Freedom.

I still remember vividly the sight of the F-14s and F/A-18s lifting off the deck, fully armed with missiles and bombs, only to return later without a single one still onboard. It left a mark. This was real. We were there to put *warheads on foreheads.* And that is exactly what we did. As an Aviation Electrician in different squadrons, keeping up systems for those aircraft to fly their missions was critical to the success we would have in our retaliation. We were the very tip of the spear, and we were showing, without a doubt, that we knew how to drive it forward.

Standing there, I watched the faint, glowing arc of Tomahawk missiles rising from the destroyers out on the horizon. And right after that, the unmistakable roar and flash of afterburners as our jets launched from the flight deck, fully loaded, disappearing into the night sky. There was a weight to that moment. It felt like everything we had endured, everything we had prepared for, had finally come to a head. It felt good to be in the Navy; not just serving, but serving with a purpose that could be felt in the thunder of every departing aircraft.

One of the hardest realizations during that time was how deeply I feared losing a daughter I barely even knew. Kathleen was living in Philadelphia then, and it felt like nowhere was truly safe. It really hit me that it was no longer just about my own survival or my own direction. I had to be present for someone who deserved a father, even if I had not been able to raise her.

That time sharpened something inside me. It reminded me that strength isn't always loud or obvious. Sometimes, it's just the steady resolve to show up, and to make things right, not only for yourself but for those who need you most.

Chapter 13
Mending Broken Ties

I was back in Florida, working in my squadron's electrical shop, and life fell back into normalcy again, except that it didn't. Unlike before, there was this hole in my heart that did not go away. It kept gnawing at me every night while I lay in bed, a deep yearning to be there for my daughter.

Even though I would drop anything and everything to go to her, I subconsciously knew that doing so wasn't possible during that time. I wasn't able to meet or spend time with her after that.

Acknowledging my lack of presence in my daughter's life was difficult, and discussing it was even more challenging, as people often only see what is on the outside, asking why I wasn't present and why I hadn't changed earlier. And I get that. But it was never about not wanting to be there. It was everything around me that kept me stuck.

My relationship with Erin had gone sour long before I got the chance to be a real presence in Kathleen's life. Though on the outside we were courteous whenever we had to be, underneath things were broken entirely through. There was no shared vision of how to proceed; there was no trust left. I still had a great deal of rage, part of it at her, part of it at myself.

And when you're shouldering that kind of burden, it overpowers everything else.

Every conversation felt like a negotiation. Every plan turned into a fight or fell apart before it had the chance to become real.

It also didn't help that, back then, staying in touch wasn't nearly as easy as it is now. Cell phones weren't a given. They were expensive, unreliable, and I didn't have the kind of money to be making long-distance calls every day. There were no video chats or quick text messages. Even the text messages available at the time cost money for each message sent.

Then there was Philadelphia itself. I could not just pick up and move there. It wasn't that simple. I had no support system. No friends, no family, no steady job waiting for me. Just the name of a city where my daughter lived, and a history with her mother that made everything feel uncertain. Showing up without a plan, without stability, would have only made things worse. I would've been a man in survival mode, trying to force something that needed patience and foundation. That wasn't the way I wanted to enter her life. I knew I needed to be steady, to offer something real and not just drop in only to fall apart again. Still, that single visit in 1998 we shared stuck with me. I held onto it like a lifeline.

Every hard choice, every quiet moment when I doubted myself, that memory gave me something to hold onto. I knew

I had missed so much already, but I refused to let that one visit be the whole story.

I didn't want to become a mere shadow who came and vanished from her life as she pleased, but I wanted to be the father I never had when I was growing up. I wanted to be the dad she could come up to when someone was bullying her or when something or someone was troubling her.

What made it so hard to connect with Kathleen in those early years wasn't just the distance; it was everything wrapped around it. Erin and I had fallen apart in every way a couple can. When I left, a heap of resentment and quiet concealed whatever knowledge we had previously. And remaining connected back then wasn't as simple as phone calling. And then there was the fact I had nothing in Philly that would allow me to be financially stable, especially the aforementioned support system.

I couldn't trust Erin or her family to help me make a life there. It's tough to admit, but although I wanted to be in Kathleen's world, I couldn't. It ate at me for years, knowing I had a daughter out there and not being able to show up the way I needed to.

However, things were different now. I knew that I was in the condition and had the resources to be there for my daughter and support her as well as myself in any way I could. Other than that, there was another reason why I was reevaluating my path in life, my own feeling of being abandoned.

Growing up without knowing my biological father's whereabouts affected me like a festering parasite, eating me up from within, even if I tried not to think too much about it. And my only way to keep this parasite at bay was to try to never be like him. So, when I looked at my daughter's picture, I knew the choice I would make then, of being a part of her life, would not just rid me of that parasite, but allow me to overcome the void I had within of not knowing my birth father.

The silent ache I had lived with, that space where a father should have been, was something I would not pass down to her. I had to break that cycle.

There were no directions or a set instruction manual that could help with forging a strong bond with my daughter, only one simple rule: Be there, be present. I made this my mantra, and carried it with me through my life, refusing to back down and disappear from my daughter's life.

It's not like the timing was perfect, either. There were still obstacles. Money was tight. The military was demanding. I had no real safety net in Philadelphia. But despite all that, something inside me shifted. I realized that showing up wasn't just about physical presence; it was about intent and commitment.

The need to be near Kathleen took root in me and started guiding every decision I made. I found myself thinking about her in the small, ordinary moments, getting gas, grabbing a bite to eat, standing watch on the flight deck. Everything suddenly carried more meaning. Even though I knew I was still trying to get my life back on track after all I had lost and still figuring out stuff, one thing I was certain of was that I needed to be nearby. I couldn't allow distance to be an alibi for absence. Once I had allowed that to happen, I almost shattered myself.

Though she still didn't know this, Kathleen had saved me a number of times. She gave me something I had not felt in years, motivating me to work harder and keep moving forward.

Making sure that I was there for my daughter, I realized that it was time for me to do what my biological father didn't: and physically be present for the daughter I didn't know.

The experience of being out there, carrying the weight of war and distance, had cracked something open in me. I was starting to realize I could not keep living at arm's length from the people I cared about, especially not Kathleen.

I stayed with my squadron, the HS-3 Tridents, for almost a year after we returned from the Gulf. On paper, I was doing my job: turning wrenches, troubleshooting circuits, and maintaining the aircraft that had just made history. But emotionally, I was checked out. I was carrying a heavier load than any sea bag; I was carrying the weight of a daughter I had spent years holding onto guilt and distance.

In December 2002, I finally transferred out of the squadron. I entered what the Navy calls a "holding pattern," waiting for a seat to open at recruiter school in Pensacola. For most sailors, a holding pattern is a time to relax, but for me, it was a countdown. Every day spent in that Florida humidity was a day I wasn't in Philly.

I spent my nights shooting the shit with Barger over dollar drafts at TGI Friday's, but even then, my eyes were on the exit. Barger and the guys were my lifeline, the brothers who kept me sane while I waited for the Navy's gears to grind forward. But by the time February 2003 hit and I packed my bags for recruiter school, I wasn't the same man who had first signed those enlistment papers. I was worn, I was weathered, and I was finally, undeniably clear in where I was headed: I was going to Philadelphia to meet my almost six-year-old daughter.

Recruiter school started in February of 2003, which was the first step I had to take in order to move away from sea duty and go into recruitment to move to Philly and be with my daughter. From that point onwards, everything I did, all the decisions I came to, were made for the sole purpose of fixing my relationship with my daughter and making up for the time I had lost.

I saw Kathleen again finally when I went to watch her play in her school's Christmas presentation, the first time since seeing her at a year old. I still remember the smell of the art supplies in her classroom. I was clumsy at first, afraid she wouldn't know me, but it warmed my heart when she called me her father and snuggled into me as soon as we met, then we became a father and daughter.

After moving in, I picked up a job as a Navy recruiter for the Navy Recruiting District situated in Philly. My station was in Marlton, New Jersey, but the work itself extended far beyond that single office. I covered a lot of South Jersey, driving to places like Fort Dix or Cherry Hill on a regular basis, and occasionally crossing state lines into Delaware or Baltimore when an applicant's situation called for it.

I even had to make a trip up to the Bronx once, just to get parental consent paperwork signed for a recruit who couldn't catch a break any other way. It wasn't a glamorous job. It was a grind most days, but it allowed me stay in Philadelphia with my daughter.

I was still living in South Philly at first, so that I could stay near Kathleen and drop her off at school in the mornings. When I eventually moved to Cherry Hill, closer to the recruiting station, I kept that same routine alive. I would still drive across the Walt Whitman Bridge every single morning to take her to school.

It didn't matter how many recruitment appointments I had lined up for the day. That drive became a quiet promise between us. The early morning was our time, and nobody could take it from us. We used to spend time before school, and my recruiting job began to unwind, talking about what homework she got, how my work was going, or simply taking in the peace and quiet as the sun rose.

But even the silence meant something: Presence. It was consistency. It was the one thing I had longed for my entire life from my own father, and now I had the chance to give it to her.

Not because of my responsibilities but mostly owing to my shy personality, my work as a Navy recruiter took some getting used to. I disliked casually chatting with people I knew, let alone approaching strangers in places like the mall or in the high schools. That stuff never came naturally to me. But I quickly discovered the job was more about honesty than it was about being polished. With actual questions, these were actual people in need of someone to tell them the truth.

And I did.

I worked so hard because I knew that every moment I honed my skills, I would get more efficient, which meant being able to spend more time with my daughter.

I didn't always get the schedule I wanted. There were days when the demands of the Navy stretched me thin. But no matter how far I had to drive or how many applicants I had to process, I always found my way back to her. In between the uniforms and paperwork and long drives, I was quietly stitching something together.

A relationship that had almost never happened. A connection that could have been lost but wasn't.

Once I got settled in with the new job, the time I spent with Kathleen became the center of everything for me. We were already growing closer after meeting again during that Christmas play, and that bond only grew stronger once I settled in Philadelphia. We grew more comfortable as we spent more and more time together, dropping her off at school every morning, going out for food. It became our thing, and we loved spending time together.

Those little moments, walking her to the car, fastening her in, and seeing her rush inside, had more significance than anybody could have probably understood. Most of that recruitment tour, my daily grounding came from those morning trips.

I could pick her up with no hassle, no long detours. I would swing by early, make sure she had what she needed, and get her to school without fail. I don't think I ever let myself miss those mornings. It didn't matter how tired I was or how hectic the day ahead looked. That time belonged to us.

On weekends, when Erin didn't have something planned

that would change the schedule, I'd have Kathleen with me. We'd make the most of it in the only way I really knew how at the time, by giving her experiences I hoped would make her smile. I'd take her to Friendly's for ice cream, let her pick her favorite sundae, and pile it high with whipped cream.

And always, without fail, we'd end up at Target. She knew the routine. Walk in, hold my hand, and then, when we got to the toy aisle, she'd get to pick out something. It wasn't too much, and it wasn't always practical, but I gave what I could. It was never about the money or ice cream, but I wanted to spoil her to make up for the years I was not there for her.

I knew I couldn't give her a perfect life. But I could give her time. The more we built those memories together, the more I believed that maybe, just maybe, we had a real chance to get this right.

Chapter 14
Hawaii: A New Start

It was 2006, three years after I arrived in Philly, and the month was March. I was moving to Hawaii for my next duty station with a helicopter squadron, the HSL-37 Easyriders. I was pretty excited to be there because it was my first time visiting the island. Even though I felt disappointed because I was traveling alone, not being able to bring Kathleen with me, I made the best of the situation as always since it wasn't really up to me. I would be deployed soon, so I couldn't bring her along with me anyway.

Still, I was looking forward to this ever since I heard stories from my former roommate and coworker, Chris. Although he was living in Connecticut for when we met, he was originally from Kauai and talked a lot about life in Hawaii.

Initially, my time in Hawaii was pleasant and quite enlightening as well. Hawaii was the kind of place that made your senses feel alive in a way you didn't quite expect. The ocean had its own rhythm, the air carried a mix of sea salt and plumeria, and the sunsets; those damn sunsets; looked like they were painted by the hands of gods. It should have been everything. In some ways, it *was* everything. And yet, I couldn't fully appreciate it back then.

I was stationed not far from Pearl Harbor at Kaneohe Marine Corps Base, Hawaii, surrounded by history and paradise, living in what most people would describe as a dream. The Navy had brought me there, and my days were filled with training, discipline, and adrenaline-charged experiences that tested every edge of me; mental, physical, and emotional. But the truth is, I wasn't in a good place mentally. I kept myself moving constantly, trying to fill every quiet space with noise, every pause with activity. I was always looking for the next best thing; the next assignment, the next thrill, the next challenge that might distract me from the nagging emptiness I hadn't yet made peace with.

There was one night in particular that I always think about. A group of us had gone out in town, nothing unusual. We hit up a local spot in Waikiki; cheap drinks, live music, and the usual laughter and banter that kept our minds off the heavier stuff. I remember stepping outside for air. The night was warm, and the breeze rolled in from the water like a lullaby. I looked out toward the harbor; just beyond the silhouettes of ships; and saw the moonlight bouncing off the Pacific like silver coins tossed across a dark sheet.

It should have been a perfect moment. But all I felt was numb.

That was the problem. You can have the best and most desirable thing or situation in your hands and not appreciate it at all if you're not well inside. That was me. I had everything people dreamed of, but I couldn't feel the joy in any of it. I was too busy reaching backward for what I had lost and forward for something that might finally feel *enough*. The present never had my full attention.

My days were full of high-speed operations and training missions for the helicopters I worked on; training to hunt submarines, boarding drills, and weapons quals. The adrenaline helped. It quieted things for a while. But eventually, even the thrill wore off, and I was left staring at myself in the mirror, wondering why nothing felt real unless it was on the edge of danger. I chased that edge like it held the answers, but I was too afraid to ask.

It took me a long time to understand that the problem wasn't where I was; it was who I was at the time. Hawaii didn't fail me. I failed to be present in Hawaii. I failed to appreciate what I had because I was still running from pain I hadn't named and regrets I hadn't released. To this day, I am still distant friends with several people from my time in Hawaii, but I never allowed myself to really get attached.

It wasn't until later; until love showed up in my life, real and honest and unwavering; that I started to slow down. I realized peace wasn't something you stumbled across in a moment of clarity on a beach or found in the chaos of a firefight. It was something you built slowly, quietly, in the stillness of finally forgiving yourself.

That kind of love grounded me in a way nothing else ever had. It showed me I didn't need to constantly strive or run or bury myself in distractions to feel okay. I could just *be.* And for the first time in a long time, that was enough.

Looking back now, I see Hawaii for what it was; not just a place but a season of my life that taught me something I couldn't learn any other way. It reminded me that beauty without peace can feel like a cage. But peace; real peace, makes even the most ordinary moment feel like paradise.

I finally learned to stop chasing regret. And in doing so, I learned how to stay still, breathe deeply, and be thankful for what I had *while I had it.*

During my time stationed in Hawaii, life wasn't always the calm, island-paced rhythm people imagine when they think of the Aloha State. While the shore offered beauty, the sea demanded grit. My time there was marked by back-to-back deployments; years where I didn't just see the ocean from the beaches but from the decks of steel warships slicing through the Pacific.

One of the more beautiful places I saw from the deck was Africa. While I technically never visited, I was definitely there.

I say technically because even though I was deployed on a destroyer, we were so close, you could say you were in Africa. I used to go up on the deck and view Mogadishu while the vessel sat on the coast of the town, watching as inhabitants of the city went about the day, taking in the scenery provided by the town buildings, and inhaling the air Mogadishu emitted, tempted to visit, but scared at the same time as the situation of the country didn't exactly make it a tourist spot, especially for us Americans.

Me on the destroyer while we did replenishment for supplies and fuel

In 2007, I deployed aboard the USS Chafee (DDG-90), a guided-missile destroyer. It was my third deployment by then, but every tour carried its own weight. Life aboard a destroyer was tight, fast-paced, and unpredictable. There wasn't much room for comfort, literally or figuratively. The ship felt like a living organism; metal and machinery stitched together with tension, discipline, and the thrum of constant readiness. We moved like a hive of ants, always working, always adjusting. I'd gotten used to the grind by that point, but that didn't mean it got easier.

The Chafee was sharp, responsive, and built for speed and precision; qualities that kept us on edge and alert, especially during operations near conflict-prone waters. We operated under high stress, always one call away from action. The kind of deployment where sleep came in fragments, and your mind never really shut off.

Just a year later, in 2008, I deployed again; this time aboard the USS Gridley (DDG-101), another Arleigh Burke-class destroyer. It was my fourth deployment, and by now, it felt like the rhythm of the sea had become an extension of my own pulse. The Gridley was newer and more advanced in some ways, but the mission was the same; project power, maintain presence, and keep watch in waters that didn't welcome complacency.

Photo I took from the flight deck of the destroyer I was deployed on. It was perfect timing to get such a symmetrical photo, and a rare occasion to see three aircraft carriers at sea next to each other.

These ships were small by naval standards, but what they lacked in size, they made up for in intensity. You didn't just serve on a destroyer; you *lived* it. The crew was tighter, the pressure higher, and the margin for error smaller. Every person on board had a job to do. We were constantly drilling and running through scenarios that ranged from man-overboard calls to missile defense, from VBSS (Visit, Board, Search, and Seizure) operations to simulated combat alerts. It was adrenaline, fatigue, and responsibility all wrapped up in steel corridors and salt air.

Those deployments were more than just rotations; they were personal gauntlets. They tested who I was, how far I could stretch, and how much weight I could carry without folding.

My time on the destroyer was tough and merciless, but it also shaped me into the person I am today. During my deployment aboard the USS Chafee (DDG-90), we spent months steaming independently off the Horn of Africa. Unlike most destroyers that fall into a battle group formation, tucked in with carriers and cruisers under the protective umbrella of layered defense, Chafee's mission was a bit different. We were out there alone, detached, and running solo. From April to September, nearly six months, we were far from home and far from support. Our homeport was Pearl Harbor, but for that stretch of time, the Indian Ocean, and the waters of the Puntland region of Somalia were our backyard. We were almost as close as when we sat off the coast of Mogadishu.

Our task was centered around intelligence-based maritime security operations. The mission was clear: Patrol those waters and deter piracy and terrorism. Back then, there was growing intel that profits from Somali piracy were being funneled into terrorist networks, including Al Qaeda. So, we were there, on the front line of an invisible war, our hull bobbing in one of the most volatile maritime zones on the planet.

Hernandez and I, with him as my safety, while I hooked up the rope to the helicopter during underway replenishment.

We found ourselves off the coast of Bargal, a small, dusty village in Puntland that most people had never heard of. But for us, it became ground zero for one of the most surreal moments of that entire deployment. We'd been holding position off that coast for a few weeks, just observing, collecting intel, and staying alert. It was the end of a long day, right around sunset, when the air took on that golden hue, and everything looked too calm to be real. My squad and I were doing something routine; grabbing rags to wipe down the helicopter and getting ready for post-flight maintenance on the flight deck.

That's when we heard it.

A sudden *boom*; sharp, deep, unmistakably close. Then another. And a strange mechanical whirring sound ripped through the sky.

We froze. Looked at each other. "Did we just fire our 5-inch gun at land?" someone asked, eyes wide.

We were facing broadside toward shore, and sure enough, we had started engaging targets inland. It was such a beautiful, peaceful scene just moments before, and now it was suddenly surreal; and more than a little unnerving.

Then the voice came over the ship's intercoms, loud and direct: "All hands, get off the weather decks. I repeat; all hands, get off the weather decks."

That order means anyone outside the skin of the ship needs to get inside immediately. But, of course, we didn't fully comply. Not at first. Curiosity outweighed caution, and from the safety of the hangar bay where we worked on the aircraft, we had just enough visual access to see what was happening.

I grabbed my Sony DVD Handycam; yeah, I still had one of those; and started filming. I grabbed one of the pilot's night vision goggles and put my camera up to it. Most of what I captured were silhouettes and smoke trails slicing through the dusk sky. Every now and then, you'd see the distant flash of impact, a small eruption of sand and fire on the coastline. We were firing incendiary and illumination rounds, lighting up the landscape like fireworks show designed for war.

We didn't have the full story at the time, but later, we found out the details. Special operations forces; just three guys on the ground; had identified high-value targets connected to Al Qaeda, and I later uncovered a video that showed one of the special operators being interviewed as well. One of the men being observed was suspected of being involved in the 1998 U.S. Embassy bombings in Kenya and Tanzania. They were trying to flee North to Yemen, and this was the moment we had to strike. And we were *there*, on station, providing naval fire support. Right place, right time.

That moment stuck with me; not just because of the chaos or the awe of naval firepower, but because, for once, we weren't miles removed, watching jets carry out the fight from afar. We were part of it, even if it was in a small, indirect way. We were on the ship, holding steady, watching history unfold in real time.

It reminded me of the strange reality of Navy life. So often, we train, prepare, and operate far from the action. We're used to watching from a distance. But that night off Bargal, we were observers no more, we were support.

It was an intense and rare kind of night, one that carved itself deep into my memory. We didn't talk much after it happened. Everyone just went back to their routines like nothing had changed, but we all knew something had. We had *done* something. Something real. Something that mattered. And in a career often filled with routine and repetition, that made all the difference.

A year later, another deployment, aboard the USS Gridley (DDG-101), we found ourselves back in familiar waters; once again deployed off the Horn of Africa, continuing the same high-stakes mission of counter-piracy and maritime security. Compared to the previous year on the Chafee, it wasn't quite as dramatic or intense, but the work was no less real. We were still chasing pirates. Still patrolling those vast stretches of open ocean where desperation and criminal enterprise collided. And still playing our part in cutting off the financial pipelines that feed terrorist networks.

Most of our days at sea followed a tense rhythm. You never really let your guard down. Every small vessel we came across was a potential threat; or, at the very least, a question that needed answering. Every unidentified boat meant launching a VBSS team; Visit, Board, Search, and Seizure. That was our standard operating procedure. We'd deploy one of the small RIBs (rigid inflatable boats) from the destroyer, loaded with armed sailors and Marines, and approach the vessel to conduct inspections. You never knew what you were going to find; sometimes, it was just local fishermen or small-time smugglers. Other times, it was something more.

That deployment had been largely routine up until the day we finally got a hit.

We intercepted a small boat; nothing that looked threatening on the surface, but something about it flagged the interest of the watch-standers. So, as usual, we launched our VBSS team. They boarded and searched, and when they came back, they weren't empty-handed. That boat turned out to be carrying pirates, along with a significant cache of drugs and cash; the kind of cargo that raised red flags immediately. It was known that proceeds from piracy in that region were often funneled directly into terrorist activity.

We detained the suspects on board the Gridley. Standard protocol. And as for the boat? Well, it had served its purpose. Now, it was a floating chunk of seized property, and we decided to turn it into a live-fire exercise target since it had no other use. We needed the training, and frankly, we didn't mind getting a little range time.

They towed the vessel out a safe distance and started with small arms fire; M4s, 9mm sidearms, and even some crew-served weapons like the .50 cals and MK19 grenade launchers. I stood back and watched, camera in hand, capturing the whole thing on my Canon Powershot G7. Still have those videos. They're shaky and raw, but they tell the story better than words.

Round after round tore through that boat. You could see it falling apart piece by piece. Holes were stitched through the side, pieces of the hull splintering off, and eventually, someone hit the fuel tanks. That's when things escalated. The tanks exploded, and almost immediately, a fire erupted. Thick, black smoke coiled up into the sky as flames spread across the deck of the abandoned boat. The fire raged for a while as everyone stood back, watching it burn like a war movie brought to life.

Eventually, the order came down to finish it off with the ship's 5-inch gun. The Gridley adjusted its position, and soon, we were watching those massive shells light up the air. The sheer force of those rounds ripped through what little remained of the vessel. With each impact, the boat rocked violently; until finally, it sank beneath the surface, swallowed whole by the ocean.

That day reminded me again how strange Navy life can be. One minute, you're sipping bad coffee in the galley, and the next, you're watching a pirate vessel explode into flames under a hail of gunfire. It's not always glamorous. It's not always dramatic. But it's always *real.* And it was just another chapter in a long line of moments that shaped the man I was still becoming.

Chapter 15
Lost and Found

When I rejoined the Navy in 2000, I was stationed in Jacksonville, still finding my footing again after everything I had been through. It was not long after that re-entry into the Navy, I would continue my journey of being lost, in 2001, not knowing the growth I would eventually experience. There was going to be lots of difficulties.

Coming home from the 9/11 deployment was a different kind of emotional experience; heavy, proud, and humbling all at once. I had served on the USS Enterprise, which was stationed out of Norfolk, Virginia, while my squadron itself was based in Jacksonville, Florida. It was a strange sort of separation; being so close to my squadron but physically part of something much bigger. The homecoming was a major event. After everything that had unfolded during that deployment, it felt like the weight of the whole country's expectations and emotions was on our shoulders. But even in peacetime, a carrier return is a huge deal. Thousands of Sailors returning from months at sea, reuniting with their families, fathers waiting to meet their recently born children for the first time ever, people standing tall on the flight deck in dress uniforms while the ship slowly edges into port; it is the kind of moment that sticks with you. I never had anyone waiting for me before that deployment. That would change though.

My mom told me she wanted to be there, to see me come off that ship in my dress blues and be a part of that moment. And true to her word, she was there, waiting on the pier in Norfolk, she took a one-way flight and rented a car. That image; her standing among the sea of loved ones; meant more to me than I probably ever let on. After the hugs, handshakes, and farewells, we climbed into a car and started the long drive from Virginia to Florida.

That trip wasn't just about going home. From what I recall, it also may have marked the first time Mom and I were alone, where it was just us that could have a conversation. I never did that as a kid because there was always Roy asking for attention, and it just never happened organically, there were always other people around. From my perspective, this was also the first time I was a part of something that I felt was the worthiest of her being a proud parent. It made me start to think more about what I had done and was going to do going forward. We all just want to make our parents proud. It just felt like a new chapter between a mother and her son.

It was about starting over in some ways. I had been living on the ship before separating from the Navy for the first time, or bunking with roommates during my early years. But this time was different. This time, I was about to get my first apartment, my own space; not shared, not borrowed. Just mine. We stopped at a Big Lots along the way, which might not sound all that special, but for me, it was a milestone. I bought my first-ever brand-new furniture to fill that little apartment on Wells Road in Orange. A couch, a table, maybe a couple of end tables; it didn't matter that it wasn't high-end. It was mine. And the fact that my mom helped me pick it out, helped me move in, and set it all up, made the whole thing even more meaningful. I was finally building something stable for once. Something grounded.

Even though I was 25 years old, that moment feels like it marked the start of adulthood in a way that all the deployments, jobs, and responsibilities before it didn't. There was something symbolic about finally having my own place, a home that did not float or move, one where I could close the door and just be. And the fact that my mom was there to help me turn four bare walls into something resembling a life meant everything. Those are the moments that change you.

Not long after that 2001 deployment, I met someone in the most unlikely of places; an online 9/11 chat forum. Those forums were basically like an early version of Reddit. The country was still raw from the attacks, and the sense of patriotism and unity felt stronger than it had in decades. We started talking about that, about how powerful it was to see people come together, and she told me how amazing it was that I'd been a part of the military response during that time. I was apparently attention seeking, and she fueled that in me.

We talked a lot, and eventually, we began what you might call a long-distance relationship. Or at least that's what I thought we were building; turned out she lived maybe an hour away, I think. Everything seemed great, until I found out she was married. And not just to anyone; her husband was also in the Navy, though at a different command. I should have had the strength to do the right thing, and walk away, but I did not. I had already fallen for her, and I did not want it to end. We were a couple of months in already so a strong connection had been made. We kept going until, eventually, she told him everything.

Eventually, we both knew she had to save her marriage, and I understood and supported that. It was one of those chapters in life that never leaves you, even when you try not to think about it. We eventually broke things off, mutually, and managed to remain friends afterward. But the guilt stayed with me for a long time. I went down the path of casual dating again, looking for that connection I needed, both a physical, and an almost spiritual thing.

A few years later, I was living in New Jersey, looking for that next connection and quickly found myself engaged to a Jersey Girl. We dated for several months before I proposed to her at a nice restaurant in Atlantic City. This was the biggest milestone I had made it to in a relationship since Erin. I had done things right this time; or at least I thought so. I even called her parents beforehand to ask for their blessing. But a few months later, I noticed something wasn't right. We used to talk for hours every night until suddenly, she was going to bed early. She had been talking to another guy from her work late at night after we would hang up, while telling me she was asleep. The phone bill was suddenly higher than normal, which confirmed it. She eventually admitted to cheating, and just like that, it all came crashing down again. Again, I turned to seeking that connection I had been longing for. That path was destructive getting exhausting, and I did not know how to get off it.

Within a month or less, I started seeing another girl; someone I had known from earlier in my life. She was my ex's friend growing up. I first met her with Shun, and he had a crush on her back then because, well, she had big boobs, and that was his thing at the time. After my breakup with her, my ex suggested I reach out to her friend, whom I saw from time to time in passing anyway. We started seeing each other casually, but I got into my own head, and the whole thing started to feel manipulative. The fact that Erin was the one who set it up after everything from our past, it started eating at me. I did not understand why, was it her guilt? It felt like another version of control, and I finally told her it was just freaking weird.

There would be other girls in my dating life, but nothing serious. I kept chasing what felt began to feel intangible. There was one that I somehow misread. I thought it was mutually "unserious", but she visited me in Hawaii a couple of times. I did not realize it at the time, but she was much more into me than I was into her. Eventually we lost touch, but I later found out from a mutual friend that she had passed away. The same friend also told me she had been in love with me. That news hit me harder than I expected. I felt like an awful person. How did I miss that? How was I so blind for nearly three years? I was the one who caused someone pain, and she did not deserve that, I was an asshole.

Looking back now, I can see how that whole time in my life was defined by a lost and found path of searching for "the one". I was in chat rooms, scrolling through "Hot or Not," "Yahoo Discrete Encounters," or anything else where I could find a hook-up. I think, in my own way, I had become addicted to that way of life, not in a clinical way that needed therapy, but in the sense that I was constantly using it to fill a void to not be alone. I was detached, floating between different connections, conversations, and they always faded too fast.

One time, I went to a woman's house expecting a hook-up, only to realize she wanted me there to make her boyfriend jealous, hoping he'd come home and catch us. That motive was not revealed to me until we were already in the act. We stopped and I left in a hurry, not wanting to get into a fight with some random guy over something I did not even want to be involved in.

Another time, a woman invited me over because she wanted to hook up even though her husband knew about it. Somehow, he was ok with it, so, I went through with it. Even now, I don't have a good explanation. I think I was just numb. That's the only word that fits. Only a couple of short years later, I was still wrecked from my divorce, still broken by the idea of not knowing my daughter, someone I had only met once at that point. I felt like I had already lost the family I was supposed to have, and instead of healing, I was unraveling. I had somehow lost sight of what Grandma had taught me about being strong and not allowing outside forces to win and take over my mind.

It all hit a tipping point eventually. I realized I was living destructively, and something had to change. I needed to stop spinning in circles and figure out what the hell I actually wanted. I would find a way.

About a year after 9/11, I learned about a chance to transfer to Philadelphia while still being able to stay in the Navy. I could become a recruiter; I could finally start getting to know my Kathleen.

I have not said a word about this until now, but during that time, I had an internal war with myself. A battle over whether I should just stay gone. She didn't know me. Maybe she was better off. Erin had married her high school sweetheart, and they were still together. He is a good man and had become a real father figure to Kathleen. I kept thinking that maybe I would just mess things up if I tried to come back into her life. That maybe disappearing was the kindest thing I could do.

But I could not, would not do it.

I thought about my own biological father. The one who left my mom when she got pregnant with me. The one who was never there. I couldn't be that man. I wouldn't let that cycle repeat. I thought about my grandma at 37 years old, still searching for her own mother, who gave her up at birth. I didn't want to imagine Kathleen going through that, searching for me, or even worse, just giving up and not caring. I thought about my mom, who convinced my dad to move our family to Alabama to get to know my Grandpa James, whom she had never known.

So, I finally reached out to Erin. I told her my intentions. I asked if she would support me in trying to get to know our daughter. And she did. We arranged a meetup soon after.

Kathleen and I meeting for first time since she was a year old, December 2002.

The first, substantial time I spent with Kathleen was during her kindergarten Christmas play. It was the first time since she was a baby, and she was aware this time. I will never forget the way she curled up against me in that school auditorium or the way she looked up at me and said, "You're my father." I still have that photo of us. That little girl snuggled into my side, smiling, knowing exactly who I was. It was the moment I realized how close I had come to missing everything.

Of course, not knowing in that moment, that little girl would grow up to be the woman who would eventually make me a papa. And in that moment, during that school play, everything shifted. I had been lost, running from pain, from regret, from myself. I was being a selfish shit full of self-pity. But now, I had something to fight for again; someone to become.

And I did; one decision at a time.

Those decisions are the ones that allowed me to begin to find myself again. Coming back into the Navy, that landmark deployment, all the moments losing myself - I was starting to believe that I had found myself. But it was moving to Hawaii in 2006, where my awakening started to reveal who I was becoming and who I am today.

When I first moved to Hawaii, I lived in the barracks with a "ghost", just a name on the door that was supposed to be a roommate, and a bed that was never slept in. I lived in the barracks for 9 months, and not once did I ever see this roommate.

I often used to wonder where he was and if he even existed, but I was getting a space meant for two people all to myself, so I just left it alone. Then one day, I realized I couldn't do it anymore, live in the barracks. It was time to move off base again. I learned how much money I could get for housing allowance and COLA, or cost of living allowance. I looked for a few weeks and found the spot, and moved in immediately.

I had a modest cottage on Oneawa Street. 500 sq ft, it looked aesthetically pleasing, and above all, I was on my own again, without any alleged roommate who could pop in at any moment. Plus, it gave me more freedom to hang out with the few close friends I had made during my stay in Hawaii. This was a first for me since I didn't have the opportunity to make good friends, except for the ones I made in the Navy, due to transferring every two or three years and having a chance to settle somewhere. In fact, this was the longest I lived in one place since moving at age thirteen; by then, I had already lived in five states.

When I wasn't deployed, life back at the squadron in Hawaii could be described in one word; exhausting. Civilians think the real stress only happens when you're out at sea, but the grind at home was often more brutal. I was often clocking in 18-hour days, sometimes longer, especially during periods of heavy maintenance or readiness cycles. Those were the kinds of weeks where you'd lose track of time, where the sun came up just as you were racing home to beat it.

I typically worked mid-shift, which meant I'd leave the squadron sometime in the early morning hours, just before sunrise when the rest of the island was still asleep. I would get home, crash on the couch or bed, depending on how tired I was, and maybe fire up the Xbox or PlayStation 3 for a little decompression, then crash hard. Wake up, rinse, repeat. That was the rhythm until the weekend, unless I had a duty section. A loop of fatigue, digital escapes, and just enough sleep to function. However, sometimes, there was a change in the usual routine when I called Kathleen, or she called me. With a 5-hour time difference, or 6 hours with daylight savings since Hawaii doesn't participate in that, it wasn't often. But it was an escape from the mundane, which I liked. Some of the calls would be brief; she would say *my ear is getting hot.* This was the signal that she was done talking. It was so cute.

On the weekends, if I wasn't catching up on rest, I tried to create little rituals; simple things to bring some sanity into my life. I would head over to Dave & Buster's in Honolulu for a cold beer and bar food. After that, I'd usually walk next door to the movie theater, catch a flick, and let myself get pulled into someone else's story for a couple of hours. But my personal slice of heaven was when I would drive out along one of the coasts with my camera. It was my therapy; driving until the noise in my head quieted, stopping to snap landscape photos, or just sitting on the beach to watch the surfers ride waves. I never had the balance or courage to try myself. That became my form of stillness.

Sometimes, I'd meet up with coworkers and hit the bars in Waikiki or downtown Honolulu, but more often than not, I flew solo. The fatigue from the week left little room for a deep connection. I was always tired. I was always just trying to exist through the cycle.

One of the few bright spots in that phase of life was not just another coworker, but my friend and mentor, Brandon. We were peers, but he was a rank ahead of me, someone I looked up to and learned a lot from. He was always happy it seemed, so his positive energy was something helped keep me going. We had been in the Navy about the same amount of time, but he had picked up a rank a little quicker. Brandon had this way of creating space around him that felt like home. He and his wife Teri would have parties at their house on base. Nothing wild; just good times. There would be a bunch of us from our shop at the squadron. We would crank up Guitar Hero and jam out with his kids, drink beers, no beer for the kids, of course, talk about life, and laugh until we were hoarse.

Eventually, like so many other unfortunate couples in the military, Brandon and Teri went through a divorce, and he transferred to a recruiting tour in Texas. Life moved on, as it always does, but a couple of years later, we heard the news that stopped everything: Brandon had been shot and killed in a murder-suicide by a girlfriend. That hit hard. A man who had once been so full of life; gone, just like that. It was another reminder of how thin the line between calm and chaos can be.

It was sad, but I didn't let it bring me back to where I was in the past, I kept moving forward.

Outside of work, my hobbies kept me tethered to who I was. Photography, especially landscapes, became a way for me to reconnect with something real and quiet. I also loved going to the movies; like, really loved it. I practically lived in the theater on weekends, and bought so many movies; DVD, VHS, Blu-ray, it didn't matter. At one point, my collection had grown to over 2,000 DVDs. They took up an obscene amount of space, so I eventually sold most of them. It made sense. Digital movies were starting to become the norm, and I needed to downsize. Still, letting them go felt like parting with memories. I managed to keep several from the collection, what I personally considered classics.

Besides movies and games, I also had a thing for collectibles. Sports cards, comic books; those were staples of my off-duty life. I even still dabbled in drawing, something I'd loved since I was a kid; it was about losing myself in the process. About translating a moment or a mood into something that stayed still on paper, even when my life could not.

There were also a few memorable adventures. One that stands out above all was when a friend and I decided to go skydiving at Pacific Skydiving on the North Shore. That moment when you are free-falling 14,000 feet over the island, with the ocean stretching out like a blanket of blue beneath you; it made the stress, the fatigue, all of it feel miles away. Literally, it was one of the rare moments I felt weightless, both in body and spirit. It just seemed so quiet underneath my parachute. I still have the certificate to prove it, because I will NEVER do it again! I feel mortal now days as compared to when I felt indestructible back then.

But for the most part, everyday life in Hawaii was boring. It was not in a bad sense; just repetitive. Wake up, grind, try to squeeze in something fun or peaceful, then do it all again. I was always running on fumes. But in that routine, I was also trying to hold onto who I was outside the uniform. It was also very isolating from my family in the mainland, too expensive for them to come see me, and I couldn't always take leave to go see them, usually just a couple of times a year.

In hindsight, I don't think I realized at the time just how tired I really was. That kind of exhaustion; mental, emotional, spiritual; does not always hit you until much later. You think you're just going through a phase, but sometimes the phase becomes your life. That's what Hawaii was for me: a beautiful place where I quietly unraveled while trying to hold it all together.

And yet, I also found moments of joy. Quiet ones, fleeting ones; but real. And in a place surrounded by paradise, sometimes that was enough to keep going, but everything has its end.

Chapter 16
An Unexpected End to Hawaii

In the Navy, everything works on a rotation. Every few years, like clockwork, you pack your gear, say your goodbyes, and get shipped off to wherever the needs of the Navy decided to send you next. My rotation was supposed to happen around March or April of 2009. I had already spent a good amount of time in Hawaii, and I was gearing up for the next chapter. My bags weren't packed yet, but mentally, I was already halfway gone.

As my time in Hawaii finally came to a close, I found myself caught in that strange middle ground between relief and regret, a feeling that can only be described as bittersweet.

After three years on the island, I had developed what people jokingly call island fever, that creeping restlessness that comes from living on a rock in the middle of the Pacific for so long. The paradise starts to feel smaller, the roads feel more familiar than comforting, and you start to crave new sights, different air, and a different kind of pace. I was ready for a change. I felt it in my bones. I needed movement again. However, as I soon came to realize, I wasn't going anywhere any time soon.

Everything was going in a routine fashion. My transfer date was approaching, and I was gearing up to leave, but then came the budget freeze.

The government had hit a pause on spending across the board, and that meant the Navy stopped processing transfers. It was a sudden stop. Just like that, everyone on the move was told to stay put, including me. At first, I was frustrated. In the Navy, change is something you brace for, something you rely on to reset the clock. I had already started looking ahead, and now I was stuck in a holding pattern with no clear timeline and no real answers.

What I didn't know at the time was that delay, that freeze, would become one of the most important moments of my life.

In total, I ended up staying in Hawaii for 3 years and 9 months. Looking back, it was more than just an assignment. It was a chapter that shaped me. Had the transfer gone through as scheduled, had I left Hawaii in early 2009, it is possible I wouldn't have the life I have right now. That thought still hits me sometimes, how close I came to missing something that would change everything.

At the time, that freeze felt like an inconvenience. Just another bureaucratic slowdown in a system full of them. But now I know that it was exactly what I needed to happen. It gave me time I didn't know I needed. It gave me *her*.

Chapter 17
Falling in Love

I had arrived in Hawaii just as I was turning 30, stepping into a new decade of life with the same emotional weight I'd carried through my twenties. Regrets, mistakes, unanswered questions, things I hadn't unpacked yet. Back then, I was still chasing distractions, always looking for the next thing that might make me feel something. But when a girl named Rachel showed up in my life, everything began to slow down. It didn't fix me, but it started something. A shift. A chance to feel grounded.

It all started when Shun planned a trip to visit me out in Hawaii. He brought Rachel with him, and if I hadn't still been on the island, we would've never crossed paths. We might have never spoken, never gotten to know each other, never gotten married. Just one government freeze, one unexpected pause in a career built on movement, made all the difference. A difference that was rooted much farther back to my earliest days in the Navy.

This is a long story, and to better explain this, I would have to wind back time to the beginning.

It started in Philly with one of my best friends at the time, Kevin. I was in "A" school when I met Kevin. "A" school was just the Navy's version of a technical school, and this was where we were learning different skills that would teach us the specifics of our jobs. This "A" school was for HT's, or Hull Maintenance Technicians, to learn our jobs. School was in South Philly, just outside of the once-famous Spectrum Arena. The Rocky statue was outside the Spectrum before they eventually relocated to the Philadelphia Art Museum. Anyway, school would teach us how to weld with gas or electricity, do fiberglass repairs, pipe fitting, hole patching for the ship's skin, and sheet metal work, among other subjects.

School started bright and early, or not so bright really, because it started before dawn. We would all get up, get in our uniforms, and walk over to the galley, where we would get a pretty decent breakfast. Sometimes they served my favorite breakfast at the time, cream chipped beef, or 'shit on a shingle' as it was affectionately known.

After breakfast, we would all line up to get in these trailers that we called cattle cars. Dozens of us would pile on and stand there while we rode to the schoolhouse across the base. I still remember riding under Interstate 95 just as the sun would start coming up. When school let out in the early afternoon, Shun and I would hang out together, looking for anything to pass the time somewhere in South Philly. If I wasn't with Kevin, I was hanging out with Shun, another close friend at the time. Sometimes, there would be groups of us all hanging out, wandering the city until curfew. Shun, and I would eventually get pretty tight, as Kevin and I would also eventually grow apart.

Shun, as we all knew him, was actually Rayshun. He said he was originally from Minneapolis, Minnesota, the same city as my future wife (although neither of us knew her yet), so I thought that he would be assigned somewhere near his hometown. It actually turned out he was from Chicago. Don't get me wrong, I would've felt happy for him if that had happened, but at the same time, if we both got orders to report to different countries, I would've felt sad to part ways with him so soon. However, as it was revealed, fate wasn't done with us anytime soon.

After graduating from tech school, 6 months later, we were both pretty ecstatic after finding out that we had all gotten the same orders to Groton, Connecticut. There were 17 of us actually going there. The dream team was not going down! He had been given work in a lag shop that mainly involved installing, removing, and replacing insulation from piping systems, while I was in the pipe shop. It was a bit different from tech school, where we had the same classes and hung out almost all the time, but it was still better knowing that he wasn't thousands of miles away; he was just a couple of hundred feet down from me under the same giant roof with all our shops, R-1 Division. If you have ever watched the movie "Down Periscope", at the beginning, there is an aerial shot of the Naval Submarine Base, New London, where they were stationed.

If it were up to me, I would have roomed with Shun in the barracks, but roommates were randomly assigned, so I was assigned a room on the third floor with Kevin, while Shun bunked with Gary. Kevin and I were still pretty close, so it was cool to have a familiar face as my roomie. I have to admit, Shun lucked out here since Gary was our mutual friend, and they were more alike than Kevin and I.

Kevin used to listen to different music than I did; he loved bands called Tool or Skinny Puppy, while I was more into Journey or Foreigner. Still, we both understood that we would be spending time together for a considerable length of time; therefore, getting to actually know one another would be for the better since we had never lived together before. We grew to appreciate our differences. Fortunately, Kevin was rather laid-back, hence it did not take long to break the ice, and before I realized it, we had become quite close buddies.

However, it was definitely awkward when it came to hanging out since Kevin didn't really interact with Shun and, thus, was not friends with him. However, to avoid this, I used to hang out with them separately, at least until the friendship between Kevin and me eventually fell apart, and there was tension between us after our falling out over Erin.

Over time, I started hanging out with Gary as well, and since Shun was also great friends with them, there was no awkwardness, and it was just the boys hanging out every night. I still remember stopping by their room, and I was sure they were watching the movie Friday, like every damn day!

Now, Shun had always been a gem of a person. He certainly had his faults, like his selfish and self-serving inclination, but ultimately, he was a nice man who was always there for me, and that is all that counts. He came to my rescue more than a couple of times, even when I had gone AWOL from the Navy unannounced, and just as surprisingly, came to his door, asking for his help. Erin and I had just gotten married and had nowhere to go and no money to find some place to settle, and since I was on an unauthorized absence from the Navy, I couldn't count on them as well. So, cornered and desperate, I turned to Shun, who had no idea where I was or what I was up to.

Yet, despite all that, he helped me, no questions asked. He was living with his girlfriend, Paula, at the time, and opened his home to us until we got back on our feet and found a place. Several years had eventually passed by this point, and Shun was like family to me, to the point that one of the running jokes was that he would most probably be our daughter, Kathleen's, godfather when she was born.

Eventually, I was back in the Navy with a suspension, and after a few months, Erin and I would move out of our apartment when I was transferred out of Groton, but even though I was no longer near him and all we had in terms of communicating with each other was the occasional letter or two, I knew that we were still buddies and that would never change, because that's just how close we were.

Just like that, years passed by with little to no contact, and I moved from state to state as part of the Navy. Around eight years had passed when I was pleasantly surprised in Philly, where my path crossed with Shun's again. You might think that after eight years of minimal contact, there might be an air of awkwardness when we first met, but it was far from it. We picked up where we left off without missing a beat.

Shun had been out of the Navy for a while now, and he was currently living with his girlfriend Rachel at that time. However, calling Rachel his "girlfriend" would be a bit of a stretch, to be honest. They had a very complicated relationship from the very beginning, dating on and off for years. After a couple of years of breaking up and then getting back together, they had realized that the foundation that their relationship was built upon was convenience rather than love and intimacy.

I always loved Shun like he was my brother, but as I said before, he had his flaws. Rachel wanted to kick him out, but she didn't have the heart to do so. Whenever she did muster up the courage and tried talking to him about it, he threatened to harm himself, triggering Rachel's past trauma, which is why she used to drop the matter in the hopes that one day he would change.

After hanging out for the first time in years, and in Philly on top of it, where it all started for us, we made it a habit to do this from time to time. I used to take a trip to Philadelphia at least once a year to visit Kathleen, and since Shun had the means, he would hop on a plane from Minneapolis and meet up in Philly. This is, coincidentally, also how I met Rachel, the girl whom I didn't know yet, but I would spend the rest of my life with. The year was 2008, and we met up to hang out as usual. I had flown out to Philly for the terrorist trial, and Shun had taken a trip here as well. Dr. Dog was playing a concert at the Starlight Ballroom on November 28th, so we decided to catch it, which was pretty fun.

The show was late, and we both had flights super early in the morning, so we decided to try to stay up all night. After everything was over, we were just chilling, talking about stuff, when Shun suggested calling Toini and Rachel, and that was when I saw her. On the call, she was acting very goofy and nonchalant, but there was something beyond that which I could not put my finger on. The conversation was not that long, but I soon realized that I had fallen and that, too, *hard.*

After the call, Shun and I spent some time together, and after a couple of hours, it was time for me to go back to Hawaii, where I was stationed at the time. I damn near missed my flight because I passed out late, or early, however you want to look at it. But throughout the entire flight, as well as on the way back to my cottage in Hawaii, I was only thinking about her.

After settling in, a few days later, I decided to hit her and Toini up on MySpace, and we talked from time to time, unaware of the surprise that was being planned in the background. Shun showed up with a surprise trip to Hawaii.

He brought Rachel and Toini with him, and true to his style, I found out barely a day ahead of time. They landed right before Rachel's birthday, May Day, coincidentally, also Shun's birthday, which, as our daughters only recently figured out, was the first of many "29th birthdays" she would keep celebrating. What he didn't realize was Rachel had already caught my eye from those first video chats the year before. Unlike so many years prior when I missed asking Erin out first, my shyness wasn't going to stop me this time.

I picked them up from the airport. My first impression of her was that she was incredibly hot. I brought them back to my little cottage in Kailua, where we drank, played music, and just settled in. Later that night, we walked down to Board Riders, a bar I loved in downtown Kailua, and had an amazing time. I could tell then that there was something different about Rachel. She wore an orange top and white pants, and looked absolutely stunning, but there was something more than physical attraction. The connection was instant and easy. To this day, it is still just so easy.

Back at my place, everyone eventually went to sleep, but Rachel and I stayed up, still talking and laughing. That night, a lot happened. We talked the whole night, me opening up about my father, my life in the Navy, and Roy, while she talked about her divorced parents, her traumas concerning her brother

Brandon, and her younger brother Gavin, who had taken his own life not so many years prior.

During that night, she also talked about her relationship with Shun. She found it to be incredibly toxic and harmful for both of them, which is why she had to break it off. I flirtatiously offered to rub her feet; she had mentioned they were sore, and that was the night everything changed. It was our first time being close in *that way*, and I knew I had never felt that kind of bond with anyone before.

Rachel brought peace into my life in a way no one else ever had. I proposed that summer and brought her back to Hawaii. We got married at Haleiwa Beach with a priest, a photographer, and a sea turtle that appeared during the ceremony; something we took as a sign. That day marked the start of everything. Since then, we have built a life together through military moves, raising our daughters Ava and Everly, and facing every challenge life tossed our way. Sixteen years in and counting, and the love is still strong.

Chapter 18
A Blow to the Gut

By the time they arrived Hawaii, I was already drawn to Rachel. We had video-chatted a few times before the trip, and there was just something about her that pulled me in. It wasn't forced. It wasn't planned. It just *was*. She had a presence that stuck with me, even through that small phone screen, and when we finally met in person, it only deepened.

I remember the feeling of that night so vividly. The breeze coming off the ocean, the sound of music spilling out into the street, and the way everything felt light for a change. We weren't talking about work or stress or the Navy. We were just living. And for me, something had already shifted. Being next to Rachel, seeing her smile, hearing her laugh, it all felt strangely natural, like this wasn't the beginning of something new but the continuation of something that had already quietly begun.

Looking back, that night at Board Riders wasn't just a birthday celebration; it was the turning point. The moment the path I thought I was on quietly gave way to something else. Something unexpected. Something real.

And just like that, Rachel began gravitating toward me, and we loved spending time together. However, not everyone was happy with this, especially Shun.

It was strange, I thought all was going well, and figured that Shun would be glad about the recent developments in our relationship, but once he figured it out, he became extremely cranky and unnecessarily rude. I pulled him aside at one point and confronted him.

I hung out with Shun a couple of times and sensed that something was off. He never really completely shut down, but there was a shift in his energy, a heaviness in his presence that hadn't been there before. We still talked and still went through the motions, but the old rhythm between us was gone, replaced by something that felt like distance wrapped in politeness.

He finally admitted that he actually expected me and Toini to hit it off because he still had feelings for Rachel, and suddenly, it all made sense. I felt sad when I realized this and hoped to apologize to him, but I never got the chance.

When Shun, Rachel, and Toini boarded their flight back to Minnesota on a redeye flight on May 4th into the 5th, the end of their trip felt heavier than it should have. It wasn't just the typical sadness of saying goodbye to people you care about; it was something deeper, something that sat in the gut and gnawed at you. That morning, I tried. I reached out to him several times, hoping to bridge whatever gap had opened up between us.

I wanted him to understand not just the decision I had made, but the heart behind it. I needed him to know that this wasn't a betrayal, and it wasn't casual. I wanted him to hear it from me directly: That I was asking for his forgiveness, but also that I couldn't walk away from Rachel. That what we had found together was something I couldn't turn away from, even for him.

But no answer ever came.

That silence, that absence of a response, spoke louder than anything he could have said. It hit hard. Shun had been one of my closest friends, a brother in every way that mattered, and knowing I had wounded that relationship, intentionally or not, was something I carried with me.

I never went into it trying to hurt anyone. But life doesn't always offer clean exits or perfect timing. Sometimes, love shows up in the middle of the mess, and you have to decide what you're going to do with it. I had made my choice. But it didn't come without cost.

He could have told me sooner how he felt about Rachel, I would have changed the approach entirely. It wasn't until after Rachel and I had already been together, after we'd hooked up, that Shun said anything to me about it. I could understand why it might've been weird or complicated from his perspective, but the timing stood out. If there had been concerns or feelings before, they were never voiced until everything was already in motion. Sometimes, it just happens, and when it does, you have to be honest with yourself and with the people around you.

That conversation before they left Hawaii, I wanted it to be clear that this was not some fling or random decision. I told him straight up that I wanted his blessing. I looked him in the eye and said, *she is the one. I am going to marry her one day.*

There was no hesitation in my voice. I meant it. Even back then, I knew it in my bones. This woman wasn't just part of a chapter in my life. She *was* the next chapter and the next and the next, until my last breath. The real one. The one I had unknowingly been waiting to start.

It wasn't about proving anything or justifying what had happened. It was about being real with someone who mattered to me and making sure he understood where I stood and how serious I was about Rachel. I wasn't asking for permission. I was offering honesty and respect.

Looking back now, I realize that the conversation had more of an impact on all of our lives than we could ever imagine.

There are moments in life that crack you open so suddenly, so violently, that the air feels different on the other side of them. Moments that don't just hurt; they shake the entire framework of who you are. I was about to be in one of those moments yet again.

I didn't even know what was happening when it started. I just knew I hadn't heard from him, and that wasn't normal. We had drifted some, yes, but this was different. Something in my gut told me to reach out, so I called Rachel, hoping she'd heard from him, hoping she'd say he was just out or busy or off the grid for a minute.

But instead, I heard the words that shattered everything.

Rachel's voice was shaken, strained, and full of something I couldn't place at first until she told me. He had just shot himself. Right there, in her house. In the bathroom, with the door closed and Rachel standing just outside, helpless to stop it. She told me the police and investigators were still there. The house, the place where this all unfolded, was still full of the sound of the aftermath.

I couldn't believe what I was hearing. Devastated doesn't even begin to describe it. I felt like the air had been pulled out of my lungs, like I was suspended in a nightmare I couldn't wake up from.

By the time I found out, it was already over. He was already gone.

Shun had even reached out to Erin, my ex-wife, with a message. We were all once part of a tight circle, bonded by years of history, shared pain, and complicated love. That's the thing that still guts me. He texted her, but didn't reach out to me. And he did not even text Rachel; he did not need to; she was right there when it happened. They had been roommates. He was literally in the bathroom with the door closed, Rachel on the other side, knowing something was terribly wrong and powerless to stop it. At some point, before the door was shut, she saw him with a pistol held up to his chest.

That image still haunts me. I couldn't imagine what Rachel had gone through, being right there. It's the kind of trauma that doesn't fade. It just settles into the corners of your memory and waits to be remembered. I go back over that day in my head sometimes, wondering what I could've done, what I missed, if one more phone call could have made a difference. But the answers never come. Just silence.

What I know now is that grief doesn't come in a single wave but comes in echoes. And this echo? Its ripples are still present.

Losing Shun wasn't just the loss of a friend; it was the loss of my oldest and closest friend. A brother. Someone who had been part of my story for so long that it's hard to separate certain chapters of my life from his presence in them. In a life marked by constant movement, from base to base, city to city, from one deployment to the next, he was one of the very few constants I had.

I've moved around more than most. That's just part of

military life. Relationships often exist in seasons: Intense but short-lived. But Shun had been with me through it all, from the early days to the moments that shaped me into who I became. He knew the versions of me that most people never got close enough to see. So, when he died, it felt like an entire era of my life died with him.

I was crushed.

And it wasn't just me who carried that weight. Rachel was devastated, too, not just because of how close she and Shun had been but because of the pain it brought back from her past. The circumstances were hauntingly similar to how her brother had taken his own life. It was like the trauma cracked open a scar that had never fully healed.

Rachel and her brother had been close, as close as any siblings can be when they aren't estranged. He was her little brother, and no matter how grown up he became or how distant life may have made things over the years, that role never changed. You could hear it in the way she talked about him. That kind of quiet protectiveness that doesn't go away, no matter what age you are. There was love there and heartbreak woven into every memory she shared.

Rachel's brother had taken his own life years earlier. He shot himself with a shotgun in front of his girlfriend. It was a level of violence and despair that was hard to comprehend, even harder to carry. From what Rachel shared with me, he had struggled for most of his life. He battled depression and had always carried heavy emotional scars. It wasn't something she talked about often, and I never pushed. I learned early on that some pain only speaks when it is ready, and Rachel would offer pieces of her story when she felt safe enough to share them.

In a few early conversations, she would tell me how nice and happy he always seemed. That's what hit the hardest, I think, how people who seem the happiest on the outside are often carrying the heaviest weight on the inside. It's a kind of sorrow that wears a smile and fools the world. And when it's gone, you're left wondering how you didn't see it coming.

We'd talk about him sometimes when it felt natural. Never in long, drawn-out conversations, just little things here and there. And more than once, we found ourselves joking, in that bittersweet kind of way, about how her brother and my brother, Roy, probably would've gotten along great. They sounded like they were cut from the same cloth, goofy, warm, the kind of people everyone liked being around. They had this effortless way of making people feel better just by being in the room. Even to this day, our daughter Everly reminds Rachel and me of both of our brothers, with her happy personality and that grin that spells trouble every time we see it. I wish I could have met Rachel's little brother.

For myself, it became a strange comfort, imagining the two of them somewhere else, laughing, getting into trouble, being those same lighthearted souls, they were here. It was a way to keep their memory alive, not in grief, but in joy. Even when the pain was still fresh, those small connections made it easier to breathe.

I respected that. I just listened when she talked, and when she didn't, I gave her space. Sometimes, the silence says more than the words ever could.

What made everything more painful was how similar the circumstances were between her brother and Shun; two people who meant something deep to us, something deep to Rachel. Two lives were lost to the same kind of silent suffering. And this time, the scene played out in her own home. She had been on the other side of the door, helpless, just like her brother's girlfriend had once been.

The weight of watching Rachel relive the loss in such a visceral way was something I'll never forget. There's a kind of heartbreak that doesn't scream. It just settles quietly in your chest and stays there, showing up in the still moments, in the glances, in the sudden silence.

And in the middle of all that pain, we held onto each other, not as a way to fix the hurt, but just to survive it.

After Shun's death, I felt like the ground had been ripped out from under me, but I knew I wasn't the only one devastated. Rachel was traumatized in a way that cut even deeper than I could have imagined at first. Shun's suicide didn't just shake her because they had been close; it reopened a wound unhealed.

The pain of her brother's death was something Rachel had learned to live with but never escaped. And now, here it was again, a different name, same tragedy. The harrowing sound of it hit her hard as if she was reliving it all over again. I could hear it in her voice when we talked. That edge of shock, grief, and paralysis all wrapped into one. The kind of pain that doesn't fade; it just lies dormant until something wakes it up.

I couldn't just sit in Hawaii knowing she was going through that. I booked a flight to Minneapolis, where she was living, and got there on May 9th, just a few days after Shun's death. I stayed until around the 16th, doing the only thing I could think of: just being there. No one really had the words, but presence mattered more than anything. We didn't talk about marriage. We didn't talk about the future. All we knew was that we needed each other at that moment.

We spent time together, exploring the city, talking, grieving, and forming a deeper connection. Our bond grew quickly. I would fly back again later in June, and by then, I knew I wanted to spend my life with her. We talked constantly, and I sent her flowers often; earning the nickname "flower jockey" from one of her friends, Susan.

The end of my time in Hawaii was already filled with transitions, reflections, and the uncertainty of what was next. But layered on top of all that was this grief we were both carrying. Hers stretching back through family history, mine freshly torn open by the loss of someone I had called a brother.

There was something binding us together that went deeper than comfort. It started when we first connected, both of us carrying the scars of losing our little brothers, and now, in the shadow of Shun's death, that connection turned into something more profound. We had experienced a similar but very different loss at separate times in our lives, but now there was this tragedy that we shared at the same time. We weren't just helping each other grieve. We were trying to make sense of life together, trying to find light in a place that had gone dark far too many times.

I flew back to Hawaii when the visit ended, but it didn't feel finished. That week in Minnesota had cemented something between us, and I couldn't shake the need to see her again. So, I booked another trip in mid-June and flew right back.

It was on that second trip that I finally said the words I had held onto since before Shun died, the words I once told him. I told Rachel, with no hesitation, "I'm going to marry you." It wasn't about romance or timing or grand gestures. It was about truth. I knew it in my bones. She was the person I wanted to build a life with, not because we were running from pain but because we were helping each other survive it.

There was a song I played for her that summed it all up, "Then" by Brad Paisley. The line that hit me hardest was:

"I hadn't told you yet, but I thought I loved you then. And now you're my whole life, now you're my whole world, I just can't believe the way I feel about you, girl."

That verse wasn't just lyrics; it was a confession; a quiet, powerful way of saying what I couldn't put into my own words.

We made the decision not long after that to get married in Hawaii since I was still stationed there. We didn't want anything big or traditional. We just wanted it to be ours. So, we planned a simple ceremony with a priest and a photographer on Haleiwa Beach, just north of where I was living on Oahu.

Rachel and I are getting married in Hawaii.

On August 16, 2009, we stood side by side on the shoreline, with the sun setting, barefoot in the sand, letting the waves and the wind carry the weight of everything we'd survived to get there. Just the two of us, and, oddly enough, a sea turtle that crawled up onto the beach behind us during the ceremony as if nature itself wanted to bear witness. We have the photos, me in my dress whites, Rachel in her beautiful dress, both of us turning to look at that turtle, smiling at the quiet magic of it all.

Rachel and I were on Haleiwa Beach on our wedding day. A sea turtle came up out of nowhere to be a witness.

One of our photos from our first wedding, Rachel and I.

So much had happened in such a short amount of time; so much loss, but so much gained. Somehow, out of that darkness, love had taken root. And on that beach, at that moment, we began something not defined by tragedy but by hope.

Chapter 19
The Redemption Tour

By the time I had married Rachel, three and a half years had already passed since I first came to Hawaii, and even though it felt great living there, I soon became bored with my life in Hawaii. Not only that, but the constant traveling was also exhausting. After a while, the small circle you travel within starts to close in on you. Even paradise has its limits when you're longing for a deeper connection with the people who matter most.

Still, I appreciated every day I had there, especially when I had my camera in hand. Hawaii was the best place I'd ever lived for my hobby, no question. There were days I'd drive along the coast for hours, stopping just to photograph the waves crashing against lava rock cliffs or the quiet moments when the sun slipped below the horizon, and the whole sky caught fire in orange and purple. Those moments kept me grounded.

But I also knew something had to change. It was time to start focusing on what came next. I had found love, real, grounding love, and I knew that being close to Rachel was not just something I wanted. It was something I needed. Living on an island thousands of miles away while trying to build a life with someone does not work forever. My squadron was trying to get me to stay there for shore duty, but Rachel and I were so new to each other, I wanted an easier transition for her. So, I began looking at ways to get back to the mainland, not just to shorten the distance but to begin building a life where my heart was.

When I met Rachel, that all changed. She wasn't just someone I clicked with. She was the person I had always been searching for. She made the world make sense again. Suddenly, all the deployments, detachments, the miles, the moments I had been on felt like they had been leading me to her. For the first time, I felt fulfilled. Not just distracted. Not just stable. But seen. Loved. Grounded. We loved each other with everything we had, and we still do. Through all the heartbreaks behind us and the uncertainties ahead, love has remained. Solid. Unshakeable. It was what I had been looking for all along. And once I found it, I knew I had never let it go.

One of the best parts of finally being together in the same place was just how natural everything felt. Life with Rachel wasn't complicated; it was easy, comfortable, and full of the kinds of moments I'd always hoped for but never really had before. For once, love wasn't something I had to chase or question. It just existed, and we leaned into it every day.

We loved to go out and do simple things together. The kind of things that, to other people, might seem routine, but to me, were everything; going out to eat, finding little restaurants, or hitting up sports bars to catch a game over a beer and some wings, just enjoying each other's company without the pressure of schedules or deployments hanging over us. Those nights were some of my favorites. They were relaxed, real, and filled with laughter.

We also spent a lot of time watching movies, whether it was catching something in theaters or curling up on the giant bean bag at home. Rachel had her favorites, I had mine, and somewhere in the middle, we built our own little shared universe of characters and stories that became part of our story.

We spent time with her mom, who quickly became someone I respected and enjoyed being around. It wasn't one of those tense, distant-in-law dynamics. It felt more like gaining a second family. Through Rachel, I was also introduced to a whole circle of friends, people who had known her for years but welcomed me in like I had been there all along. Over time, they became our friends. We built a life that was rooted in connection, something I had been missing for far too long.

By the time Rachel and I had been married for almost two years, we found ourselves in that space where love deepens and dreams start to take root. We had built a life together. It was steady, loving, full of the kind of quiet joy that grows out of simple routines and shared hopes.

And then, we hit another milestone: We bought our first house together. That felt big. Not just because of what it meant financially, but because it was ours. A place where every wall, every piece of furniture, every little imperfection carried a piece of our shared story. It was no longer just about surviving or staying afloat. We were building something, piece by piece, together. All those things, dinners, games, friends, a home, added up to something I hadn't experienced in a long time: A sense of belonging. And that made all the difference.

I knew that now that I had a home to come back to, I finally had roots. It reminded me of why I had chosen recruiting all those years earlier. Back then, it was a strategic choice for my daughter Kathleen, it was a redemption tour. This second time around with Rachel, it was about starting our marriage off on the right foot, from the beginning, no need for second chances.

That first time, moving to the East Coast meant a chance at getting to know Kathleen when she was 5. That was when we truly began as a daughter and father. She was old enough to remember, to laugh with me, to hug me, and call me Dad. I still remember how nervous I was in those early moments. I had missed so much already. But I was there finally. And that mattered.

That first time, my role as a Navy Recruiter, it wasn't just a job or career choice, it also meant changing who I was at my core. I had always been more of an introvert. Quiet. The kind of guy who wouldn't approach a stranger unless I absolutely had to. But recruiting doesn't allow for that. If you want to succeed, you must step way outside your comfort zone and strike up conversations with anyone, anywhere, anytime. I did not use the high-pressure tactics the stereotypical recruiter used. I just talked to them like people, with honesty. I had gotten out of the Navy and reentered it, so I believed deeply in the "product" I was selling. Maybe because I was an introvert, I listened more than I spoke, and that's what those kids needed.

To prepare, I attended a 30-day Navy recruiting school. This was a crash course in salesmanship, public speaking, and human connection. It didn't take long before I started to get the hang of it. I actually became really good at it. Consistently ranked in the top 10 recruiters in the Philadelphia district, which covered Maryland, Delaware, Eastern Pennsylvania, and Southern New Jersey. I was winning awards, earning recognition as a rising star, and consistently hitting or surpassing goals, even while working in a station that didn't exactly offer much help from my peers.

I remember one moment in particular that still sticks with me. Our Chief Recruiter sat everyone down and laid it out plainly. He told them that they should be ashamed. I was the one carrying the entire station, putting in twice the effort while everyone else coasted. Not my words, they were his. He didn't sugarcoat it, and to be honest, I appreciated that kind of honesty. It wasn't about ego. It was about work ethic. And I had found mine.

Over time, I built up a list of applicants that was strong enough that I could be selective. I didn't have to take just anyone. And I am glad for that because it gave me the space to act with integrity, something I refused to compromise on.

One situation with an applicant still gives me chills, he was a young man from Cherry Hill, New Jersey, which was part of my assigned territory. Something did not feel right from the start; I caught him lying during the application process, and I immediately shut it down, stopping his processing cold. My instincts were speaking loudly to me, something was not right. Those instincts, they are the ones I had honed on the flight deck of the aircraft carrier, the ones that kept me aware of all the danger around me, was blasting in my head, but this time, served me in another area of my career outside of being on a ship.

Years later, while I was deployed in 2007, I learned who he really was. I still remember the hum of the ship as we sailed through whatever waters we were in at that moment. We were in the shop at the end of the day just completing a turn over between shifts, when I saw his name flash on the screen. It was bad, my former applicant, along with five other men, had become known as "The Fort Dix Six." They were arrested after an FBI investigation uncovered a plot to attack Fort Dix and kill as many U.S. soldiers as they could. And the reason he had tried to join the Navy in the first place? To gain access to the base. That realization hit me hard. Had I not followed my gut, had I not shut it down, who knows what could have happened?

When I returned from that deployment, I had to interview

with NCIS giving any details I may have had that could help with the prosecution of my former applicant. Looking at all those potentially saved lives, including people exactly like the sailors I was recruiting, solidified my belief that doing the job the right way was the only way to do it. With that principle, I carried my momentum forward, self-assured.

When I eventually transferred from Hawaii to Minneapolis, where Rachel was from, I brought those lessons learned from that first recruiting tour with me. And once again, I was good at it. Another recruiting district, another chance to push, and I rose close to the top there too, consistently setting and attaining hard to reach goals.

But the real reward wasn't in the numbers. It was in the people. In fact, it always went back to knowing I could possibly serve next to those new Sailors I recruited, like the two I served with in Hawaii, the same two I assisted in getting them through the recruiting process. I keep in touch with a lot of the "kids" I recruited. I watched them grow into sailors, into adults, into people with their own stories. That bond didn't just fade when they shipped off to boot camp. In fact, one of those two former recruits, Jason, is preparing to retire from the Navy in 2027, and he lives locally in the same county my family lives in. I was able to meet up with him, his wife, and little baby, where Rachel and my kiddos were able to meet the "kid" I recruited 20 years ago.

For years, I had lived a life full of movement,

deployments, relocations, high-tempo missions, and all the chaos that comes with wearing the uniform. I'd seen and done more than most people experience in a lifetime. I'd had wild nights and quiet drives, sunrises over steel decks, and late-night walks through foreign streets. Adventures, sure, but always alone in the end.

That was the part I didn't talk about much. No matter how full the days were or how loud the nights got, I'd always come home to an *empty room*. Whether I was on the island, tucked away in a barracks, or driving to little cottage in Kailua, or on my first ship where I lived, it was the same routine. After working 18 to 20-hour shifts, I'd get back to whatever space I was calling home at the time, fire up a game or two, maybe eat something quick, and zone out. It wasn't sadness, exactly. It was just a kind of emotional numbness, a daily reminder that while I was doing a lot, I didn't have someone to share it with. That emptiness stayed with me, even in beautiful places. Even surrounded by friends. Even with the distractions of rank, duty, and entertainment. I was living, but not fully.

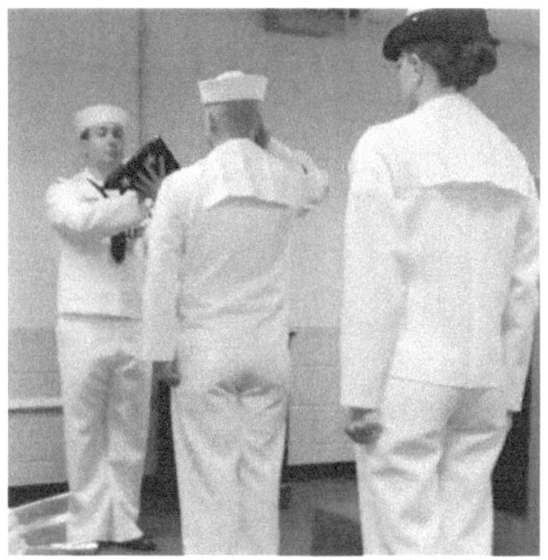

Me receiving the flag at my retirement ceremony from "kids" I recruited.

Fast forward a few years to 2015, when it eventually came time for my retirement ceremony in Norfolk, Virginia, three of them showed up. That blew me away. One of them was the first person I had ever recruited. Another was the last recruit I ever signed from Minneapolis. Standing there with them, seeing their uniforms, knowing they came to honor that moment. It meant more than I can explain. It told me I had done it right. That I wasn't just pushing papers or filling quotas. I was changing lives. And maybe most importantly, I never carried that "all recruiters are liars" stigma. I never had to.

Chapter 20
Clean Slates

Rachel and I had been married a year, a year since we were on that perfect Hawaii beach by ourselves, it was now time to share our love with friends and family. On August 20, 2010, we stood together and renewed our vows, this time not just as two people promising a life together, but as two people who had already been through enough to know exactly what that promise meant. We did not want to go too crazy for the anniversary, as we had each other, and that was what truly mattered. However, we still managed to find a unique venue, which we thought was picture-perfect.

We came across a way to celebrate our anniversary at the Wabasha Street Caves located in St. Paul. To any random person, the venue might seem strange, but to Rachel and me, this old speakeasy, set into the side of a limestone hill, possessed more value and beauty than the best mansions.

The front was a façade that made it seem like any normal building, with bright green ivy growing all over it. It had a rustic charm to it. The entrance seemed more of a hidden hideout when you arrived; it screamed "wedding" in no clear way. This was not due to theatrics or us wanting to be dramatic, but it was just really cool to us.

When it came time for the vows, we didn't try to be overly polished. We let the moment be real. Our songs played, "Then" by Brad Paisley and "Halo" by Beyoncé. These songs meant a lot to us as they were an outlet to help us express our grief when we couldn't to anyone else; it felt natural for them to be included. They were the soundtrack to our life when we first met and experienced new love and loss.

Rachel and I the day of our rewedding/vow renewal a year after we were married.

As the music played, blending together, we stood, hand in hand, pouring sand into a glass vase, signifying our bond transforming from two separate people into one unit.

Another part of the cave was set up for the reception. We

brought in long tables and created space for dancing. We managed to incorporate the cave's dark and eerie atmosphere in the best way possible, setting up ambient lighting and a delectable assortment of desserts lined across the tables, all the side characters to the main dish that sat in the middle: A three-tiered cake that looked delicious as well as elegant.

This was by far the best party we had ever thrown, with people laughing, enjoying the moment, and everything just looked like a celebration where everyone was having the best time.

After the anniversary, my life with Rachel was going as well as it could. I was a year into a great start of my second recruiting tour, no worries of deploying anytime soon. We set off back to Hawaii for our honeymoon. It was a long overdue return to where we began, but maybe that made it even more perfect. It felt like the right time to take the next step. We decided to try for a baby.

It wasn't a rushed decision. It was something we had both thought about and talked through, and when we finally agreed to start trying, there was a quiet excitement between us, hopeful, cautious, but full of love. And not long after, Rachel was pregnant. It felt like a small miracle at first, it made us so happy. That spark of life, that early promise of what could be. A few months in, the miracle started to fray. Rachel began experiencing abdominal pains. We were not sure what was going on, but something did not seem right.

However, as the days went by, the pain began to worsen out of nowhere, without any triggers, and grew beyond mere contractions. Then there was the incident where Rachel experienced vaginal bleeding, which was an alarm for us. We got worried and rushed to the hospital right away, praying that it was just a minor complication and not a worst-case scenario.

After consulting with the doctor and getting a few tests done, he took some time to examine the results. It took around an hour, but to Rachel and me, it felt like an eternity. As we were sitting in the waiting room, a lot of thoughts were rushing through our heads. Helplessness. Hopelessness. The fate of our unborn child was at stake, and all we could do was sit around and wait.

After what felt like an eternity, the doctor called us back in, and the look on his face did not reflect relief or relaxation. Instead, it was intense, which was not a good sign for us. He sat us down and broke the news. As I heard him say that the baby was no more, the entire world came crumbling down around us. All of a sudden, everything went on mute. As he said the words, the world went on mute. The doctor's mouth kept moving, but I could not hear him anymore, just the roar of my own thoughts. Our bundle of joy, our blessing, was gone. I didn't know what to feel, how to feel, how to work through this and process this.

Both Rachel and I were absolutely shattered. The news came to us at light speed, giving us no time to process anything.

Of course, personally, I was sad, even more so because I knew Rachel also wanted a baby, her first baby. I had always said to myself I would not have any kids after Kathleen. It took a lot of time to foster and maintain a strong bond with her after what I did to her, and I always thought that she would be my only child. However, one day, Rachel and I were talking about something, I don't even remember what it was, when out of the blue, the topic of mothers came up.

I never really knew Rachel's point of view relative to my own in terms of parenthood and children, but I knew that day that it was different for her. She really wanted to be a mother.

The relationship between Kathleen and I had drastically changed from the first time we met. What began as redemption tour had transformed into love and connection, and Rachel also wanted to experience that sort of love. She loved Kathleen, and Kathleen of course loved her. Rachel still wanted to be a mother, and when she talked about this, it sparked something within me. At first, I believed that this may be more than we could take on, but when Rachel told me how much she yearned to be a mother, I figured that it would all be worth it. And if any problems do arise, we'll work through them together, as a family.

That conversation really unlocked a dormant thought within me, and I began to look beyond the family I had now, onto the thought of a newer addition, and as the days went by, my hopes to extend the family and build something new grew stronger, which is why losing those hopes and dreams was all the more crushing.

What my mind was going through was much more than sadness. The feelings that surged within my heart and soul were an incredible sadness. My environment felt numb. I felt numb. But just as hopelessness was taking over my mind, I knew I had to be there for Rachel, I couldn't be selfish, she was devastated. I took her hand in mine, it brought a sense of warmth. Her presence cut through the numbness and hopelessness that had previously clouded me, reminding me that I wasn't alone, she wasn't alone. We had each other.

Even when I recall memories of that day, there is a stinging pain in my heart. But in an instant, the pain goes away as well, because along with the loss of a loved one, I also remember how it strengthened the love between Rachel and me, serving as a remembrance of the bond we had forged between us, persevering through the bad times, and depending on each other. It's not just grief for what we lost; it's grief for what we were beginning to imagine. All the firsts we would never get to see. The future that never arrived.

We took some time off after the miscarriage, grieving together and healing. It was difficult at first. We actively avoided passing by any store that sold baby clothes and toys, as well as holding each other's hands tightly whenever we saw anyone with their baby, playing with them, or loving them.

We watched other parents playing with their kids with equal parts longing and heartache in our eyes, slowly healing. After a few weeks, we sat together and talked. Rachel and I talked about the baby and the next steps, whether we were ready, or if we should give it more time to come to terms with it.

We gave ourselves space to heal, not just physically but emotionally. There was no pressure to rush into trying again. We just leaned on each other, let time do what it could, and when we felt ready, we tried again. That's when we got pregnant again. This time, we'd get to meet the child we were already falling in love with.

After a long discussion filled with tears and smiles, we began to hope again. Determined not to give up, we kept on trying, in the hopes of being blessed with a new life, for me to become a father, and above all, for Rachel to fulfill her dream and become a mother. After months of trying, the time finally came. Hope had blossomed into determination, which then bloomed into a miracle in March 2012 in the form of little Ava Grace Thornock, our hope.

Because of our past miscarriage, we rejoiced as well as lived in constant terror after learning Rachel was pregnant. We were scared that if our past came back to haunt us, it would break us permanently, and we no longer possessed the bravery and tenacity to endure what we had seen previously. This is why we were probably the most cautious expecting parents in the world from the beginning, right till the very end. Rehearsing possible scenarios, preparing baby kits, monitoring food and nutrition intake, reading book after book about pregnancy, weekly doctor visits, you name it, we probably did it during that time.

Although I had a great relationship with Kathleen, with Ava, I had the one thing I thought I'd lost forever, a clean slate. There were no missed years to make up for, no apologies needed for being gone. I was there from the first breath, and I intended to stay. I was never forced away. Ava was a second chance to get it right from day one, to undo the ghost of the mistakes I'd made by being absent during Kathleen's early years.

Ava and I were very similar in terms of mannerisms, mostly when it came to her personality. Just like me, Ava was emotionally strong, thinking and acting with her heart rather than her mind, and unfortunately, another thing she picked from me was my short temper. And like me, she wasn't sure how to express those strong emotions. This was a harmful combination as it led to many times when Ava lashed out in anger, but that rage disappeared just as quickly.

I hadn't always been like that. The truth is, before I left the Navy, it took a lot to push me to that edge. But after service, the gears shifted. I was eventually diagnosed with anxiety, and somewhere along the way, my patience started thinning in places I never expected. That vigilance that I relied on to keep me safe on the flight line or on the deck of a carrier had somehow disintegrated into a constant, buzzing anxiety. It was all exacerbated by the never-ending ringing of tinnitus, the fucking loud ass crickets in my head just wouldn't shut up. Between that internal noise and the external world, everything suddenly felt too loud. My patience was fading.

Back in Hawaii, those long drives with my camera were how I quieted the noise. I had to learn how to find that same silence now, even with a toddler in tow.

Where I once let things slide, I found myself reacting before I had time to think. And when I looked at Ava, I saw that same pattern emerging. It was hard to face. No parent wants to believe they passed down their worst traits, especially not the ones they've been working to fix. But at the same time, I knew I had a chance to stop it from becoming something that defined her like it had started to define me.

Ava wearing daddy's boots, already stepping into my world, and reminding me why I had to work on the man standing in them.

And on the days when I wasn't at my best, when the anxiety crept in and made me impatient or distant, I tried my best to show up in other ways. I apologized. I explained. I listened when she was ready to talk. We were both still learning, still are: I, how to be a better father, and she, how to grow into herself. And in that space of learning, we found room for grace and patience in each other.

Ava showing us her artistic side.

Ava's artistic side shows in her drawings. When I told her I was writing this book, I asked if she wanted me to share anything with my readers. To her, it was just colors on a page; to me, it was proof that despite all of the noise and the anxiety, we were building something beautiful together.

Chapter 21
The Beginning of the End

It had been quite some time since I had joined the Navy, and after nearly two decades of hard work and deployments away from home and family, it was finally time for my final tour. Throughout my life in the Navy, I had been to many places, both in and out of the country, but this was the first time I had a tour in Norfolk, VA.

Standing with my daughters in front of my first ship. She was waiting for her retirement to the scrapyard, and I was still freshly retired. Two relics of a different Navy, both finally coming home.

It was an odd time though, as my last deployment came earlier than I expected. It was 2008, seven years before I would retire, and it turned out to be my fourth and final one. I didn't know at the time that it would be my last. That deployment in

2008 was an unknown milestone at the time, for more than one reason.

I was aboard the USS Gridley, and we solo-steamed the whole time doing anti-piracy ops. It was intense, strange, and one of the more memorable deployments I'd had. We detained a group of pirates; weapons, drugs, cash. Once we had them, we sank their boat. It was surreal to watch it go under. That mission gave me one last story to take with me.

But the end came unexpectedly. Something from my past was still in the shadows. The shocking news broadcast of the "Fort Dix Six" from a year prior on my 2007 deployment, came back as a surprise yet again. I got pulled early, flown home from Singapore to testify in the "Fort Dix Six" case. Because of the information I provided during my 2007 NCIS interview, I was subpoenaed by the United States Department of Justice.

My command was not happy either, since there are major inspections at the end of a deployment, and I was one the more senior Sailors on that deployment. But there was nothing they could do to stop it either. One week I was watching a pirate vessel being sunk, the next, I was sitting alone in a hotel room in Cherry Hill, New Jersey. I was tasked with giving testimony behind closed doors before federal attorneys and a judge in a Courthouse in Camden. He would go on to be sentenced to 33 years in prison. It was intense, but the upside was that I got to see Kathleen during that same trip. It was Thanksgiving, and once my obligation was done, the Navy let me stay the rest of the week with her.

For most of my adult life, I was with the Navy, either working back at home on the flight line or deployed on the ship, rinse and repeat, for almost 18 years. Although it was about time for me to retire, I was working hard so that it wouldn't happen. Don't get me wrong, I desperately wanted to retire so that I could spend time with my wife and children, but at the same time, I wanted to make some money before retirement to ensure a stable future as a family.

In the U.S. military, there is a term known as High Year Tenure, which refers to a management policy. This policy sets a restriction on the number of years you are allowed to serve at a particular pay grade, and if one does not get promoted within the time frame, they must be discharged or retire if they have accumulated enough time. For myself, I was a Petty Officer First Class, or E-6, and only had a couple of years left until I would be forced to retire, unless I made it to Chief. There were patriotic inclinations that encouraged me to stay in the Navy, but at the same time, it was also a decision I had made in order to make more money before I retired, as once you get promoted to Chief, there is a certain prestige and additional tradition that comes with it. That also means you can serve for more years, getting a generous bump in your pay grade.

In hindsight, I always had a seed of regret when I look back at leaving Philly behind for Hawaii. Not only did I leave

Kathleen, during that timeframe, advancement to Chief was basically a "gimme" in the Career Recruiting Force (CRF). While I was in Minneapolis recruiting, the odds were better than average, but never as good as that first time recruiting. If you spelled your name correctly on the 175-question rating exam, you would find a clear path to Chief's Anchors.

There were of course more boxes to check to actually get there, like EVALs, the physical fitness test, and the tangibles & intangibles found during the review of service records if you made board. It was the Navy's system to separate the doers from the strategists, and the ones just showing up for a paycheck. It also never hurt to know someone up high, which sometimes trumped everything else. Making Chief wasn't just advancement, it was a selection process. I let pride get in my way and decided I wanted to make Chief in the rating I had already been in learning and living.

That decision put me directly in the crosshairs of High Year Tenure. As an E-6, I was staring down a deadline: get promoted or get out. I arrived in Norfolk with only two attempts left and a massive disadvantage. I was stepping onto a flight line filled with a brand-new version of my old helicopters, a version I never worked on, while my brain was still wired for recruiting.

There was one maintenance gripe that needed troubleshooting, and I thought to myself, I have seen this issue before when I was in Hawaii. I walked out to the aircraft confident, with the Toughbook containing the maintenance manual in hand. I quickly realized that the junction boxes that once occupied the sides on the outside of the aircraft I knew, were now inside the cabin of an aircraft I didn't know as well as I thought. I was fighting to prove I still belonged in the on the flight line after three years away.

I knew I had to impress the senior officials to get great enough evaluations and get endorsed to be promoted, and the best way to do that is to show them that you aren't just a foot soldier, but a leader. On top of it all, I didn't have as much time as most of my younger peers who were all working towards that same goal. Most of them knew there was "always next time." I knew that I had to work harder than ever if I wanted to secure a promotion before the end, so I took on multiple extra duties that were out of my comfort zone. There was no time for living comfortably, and I knew that I had to take risks in order to prove to my higher-ups that I was capable of leading efficiently, which is why I prioritized leadership roles rather than keeping a low profile and working behind the scenes.

The junior Sailors in the shop would not make it easy either. There was one incident where the night shift had checked out a piece of gear that is used to load certain codes into the aircraft's communication systems. There were certain protocols that had to be followed because those codes are classified. So, two Sailors always had to be present while carrying it. When it wasn't used, it was supposed to be in a safe. It turned out two Sailors had just left it in the hutch above the desk in the shop, unlocked, unsecured, with no one knowing it was there, a huge fuck up. I hadn't even been in charge for a month when this shit happened, but as a senior Sailor, it happened under my leadership, no excuses. My leadership team was not very happy with me and removed our shop's qualifications to use that gear until everyone was retrained.

There was a lot of pressure on me since my years were about to be up, and I only had one tour left, but it wasn't all bad. For one, I was quite lucky in terms of timing, since you are able to retire regardless of your grade or whether a mandatory retirement or discharge is in effect or not, once you serve for 20 years or more. Normally, this might seem like bad news, but for me this was good since I wanted to retire as soon as possible and if I were to get promoted beforehand, I wouldn't have to serve much time as an E-7, and could retire in the fraction of time while being able to redeem the pay rise and other long-term benefits which come with becoming an E-7 as well. However, this was *if* I could get promoted, and I was working tooth and nail to turn this *if* into a *when.*

It was pedal to the metal every time, all the time, as soon as I arrived. I had even gotten qualified as a Phase Coordinator, the same role I qualified for in Hawaii. It was a big deal because there were not many Phase Coordinators.

From leading training sessions and work centers to performing as a quality assurance inspector, I made sure that all my free time was occupied with leadership duties. I had a goal, and there was no stopping me any time soon. Other than the usual extra duties, I also volunteered for the position of a Duty Section Leader. This required me to instruct a team of sailors who were assigned to me by the squadron in order to fulfill various tasks, such as performing cleanups around the squadron, standing watch, and also staying longer than normal times. Some of those longer hours were when a helicopter required extra maintenance to get ready for missions, and the duty section would assume the extra activity in order to ensure that all the other non-duty personnel were able to leave at reasonable times.

If it sounds exhausting, then you are right, it was, both physically and mentally. However, thankfully, we were not on duty all the time, but only four days a week.

Time went on, and the gruesome, draining weeks went by much slower than I would've liked them to, but I did not let on or slow my performance. In fact, week after week, I grew more efficient in leadership and management, working hard day in and day out, hoping that my dedication would be noticed, and it was not in vain. After a couple of months, I had grown into a Duty Section Leader to the point where I had increased my leadership and management of my team of sailors, and one fine day, I was promoted to a senior Duty Section Leader. The new designation made me noticeably happy since it meant that the hard work I was putting in was being noticed; technically, it was more of an assistant to the senior section leader since a Chief typically held that role, but it was often delegated it to a responsible and senior E-6.

I was now in charge of multiple Duty Section Leaders. The long hours as a Duty Section Leader meant the tinnitus 'crickets' in my head were screaming by Friday, but seeing Ava and Rachel every day, and walking through the Botanical Gardens would help quiet the noise and ease my anxiety a little.

From there on, I went on to become a Command Urinalysis Coordinator. In that role, I was selecting a certain percentage of the sailors at random to test for drugs, as per the instructions set forth by the Navy. Everyone was subject to authority under the urinalysis program, all the way up to the Commanding Officer. While not a glamorous role, it was one of the most authoritative roles an E-6 could hold, with much responsibility.

The reason why I took on this role was that, even though it may sound unnecessary, it was a pretty valuable role in the Navy, and I had to do many other tasks other than simply drug testing sailors all day. Once again, I was moving up the hierarchy, improving my evaluation and bringing me closer to the promotion, but a higher position in the ladder also meant more responsibilities. As a senior E-6, we were often sitting on boards in charge of selecting junior sailors to be given awards for their hard work, as well as preparing evaluation reports for the sailors under our mentorship.

As the tour went on, I had pretty much covered every

position as an E-6, but not everything. The only thing that was left was for me to be a first line supervisor, or Leading Petty Officer (LPO) at sea, and that was a challenge because, even though I had a versatile skillset and experience as a shift supervisor and an LPO for my squadron in Hawaii previously, that was for what we called Homeguard. Homeguard was everyone not currently deployed, and the remaining aircraft not deployed, typically around 12 helicopters at any given time. Unlike the other positions I had obtained previously, I did not have the right network in place, which would have put me in a more advantageous position.

Thus, even though I requested to be deployed as an LPO, it was all for naught. I started as an LPO for the Avionics shop, as well as an assistant LPO for the QA shop, but there were people being groomed within an already established network, one that I was not a part of yet. After spending some time getting familiar with the workflow and my everyday jobs, I was eventually moved to the Hazardous Materials department, where I was the manager and supervisor, along with retaining my role as an LPO for the tool room. Some might view that as a demotion, but no matter what I was tasked with, I put pride into it and worked to be my best.

It didn't take much time at all to understand the work involved in the tool room, QA shop, or the Avionics shop; the same can't be said for the Hazardous Materials department. When I became the supervisor and manager of the department, it was run very well by one of my peers, but I found inefficiencies that could make it even better. I made some great improvements, with my most notable achievement came during a Navy Occupational Safety and Health inspection. I do have to give credit to my friend and peer, whom I replaced in the position; she had been doing very well in turning it around, I just took it the rest of the way.

It was tough at first, but work only got better as time went on, with huge help from my wife, Rachel, who took over as an OMBUDSMAN for the squadron. She was the official representative of my squadron's Commanding Officer and was vital in maintaining current and accurate communication between the deployed command members and their family members, and it was a precious role. Not only that, but it gave her something to do while remaining close to me, and I would be able to spend time with her as well, making this a win-win for both of us.

Another reason why Rachel's presence came at such a good time was that, at the time, she was not doing so well. She tried to find work, but the math never added up. Any income she might bring in would have been eaten up by childcare, and in the end, it would have cost us more than it gave. So, she stayed home, doing her best to manage the household with a toddler in tow and very little adult interaction outside of her OMBUDSMAN responsibilities. It wore on her. I could see it, even if she didn't say it out loud.

Rachel was not just a spouse waiting for me to come home

every day; she was the lifeline for every other family in the squadron, even while she was struggling with the isolation herself. Our life in Norfolk was busy and incredibly tiring, both mentally and physically. It gave us more time together than we might have had otherwise. Most days started early and ended late, and between duty, inspections, and my college coursework, I barely had anything left in the tank by the time I walked through the door. But I still carved out every moment I could for Ava. That little girl had a way of resetting everything in me, even when I was running on fumes. I would read to her every night and sit with her until she fell asleep before placing her in the crib.

With this, hours became days and days became weeks until, finally, the time to get the fruit of all the hard work, blood, sweat, and tears I had put in always came down to my performance evaluations. That ship had figuratively sailed before I even got to where I was. A previous division chief had sealed my fate the year prior.

During an evaluation when I was working in the Quality Assurance shop, the division chief started off by asking me a question that knocked the wind out of me, which was, "How many more times do you have left to make Chief. You still have a few years left before you are up for retirement?" This was incredibly alarming because during a sailor's evaluation, you needed to understand the sailor's goals, and the fact that he asked me this question meant that he didn't bother to look at my service record, which could only mean one thing: There was no chance to get promoted. Even though I did not get promoted at the time, life wasn't all doom and gloom. I would manage to find the silver lining in my situation, it's all I could do, and I did not want the negativity to affect my family.

Rachel and I always managed to find time to step out of work and do family stuff. We would walk through the Norfolk Botanical Gardens or let Ava burn off energy at the indoor playground downtown. We even tried ice skating once.

I was terrible at it, but Ava loved it, and Rachel laughed, and that was enough. When my dad invited us to Mexico to visit him and his third wife, Angelica, all expenses paid, we naturally jumped at the chance. Rachel and Ava finally got to meet my dad and the rest of his family out West, and it was worth every minute.

Later that same year, we all drove to Gatlinburg, Tennessee. Kathleen came too, along with my mom, Curt, my stepbrother John, and his family. My mom rented a beautiful cabin in the woods for all of us. That's really what Norfolk became for us: Not perfect. Not easy. But we did what we could with what we had, and we made the good moments count.

Chapter 22
End of An Era

About a year had passed since my interview with the Chief, who didn't even make the effort to get to know me or know where I was in my career.

Still, I kept working on myself while going through other leadership positions and collateral duties that no one wanted to do. Even Rachel had stepped outside of her comfort zone when she became the Command Ombudsman. We remained optimistic for that final chance at advancement until it was out of reach. The hourglass had dropped its final grains of sand, and before we knew it, months had gone by in a flash when I decided that it was time to put in my request for retirement. I realized that grooming those younger Sailors was the priority, and my time on the flight line was officially drawing to a close.

At the same time, Kathleen was approaching 18, preparing to graduate from high school, and was getting ready to start "adulting," while Ava was coming up on three. Watching my children grow became a factor contributing to the consideration of retirement. I didn't just randomly wake up and make an impulsive decision to retire, but had been thinking about it for a while now, not to mention high year tenure was sneaking up. I knew that I would have to hang up the uniform sooner rather than later.

I wanted to keep Rachel in the loop about taking such a big step because I loved her and valued her opinion as well. So, I first had a long conversation about this with Rachel, laying out my thoughts and final decision regarding retirement. She had been so supportive of our short time together, married while in the Navy, that I wanted her to be integral to the process. Thankfully, she was incredibly supportive of everything. I had already gathered enough experience and accomplishments during my time in the Navy to rack up enough benefits to not worry about a pension for the rest of my life, so Rachel was alright with it. We started planning where we wanted to settle down and move.

During all of this time in Norfolk and having not visited Hawaii ever since our marriage or honeymoon, we didn't see that as a feasible option. Although we made some sweet memories of that place and at one time, it felt like a second home, but now it was time to close that chapter, and of course, we knew it would not be beneficial for us financially in the long run. I mentioned the Florida Gulf Coast to Rachel, close to where I grew up. My mom and Curt were also looking at moving back down South at the same time, so we assumed a support system would be in place if we moved to Florida.

So, after thinking about it for a little bit, we decided to make a plan that included Florida. We were excited for this new chapter of our lives, being there for Rachel, Kathleen, and Ava. Earlier in 2014, I attended my first TAP Class, or Transition Assistance Program, in Norfolk. It's a benefit that all service members are entitled to. It's a workshop that helps to ease the burden of transitioning from military service to the civilian workforce.

I learned a ton, how to network and what to do. Things like translating my military experience into civilian equivalent jobs. After a week in that class, I quickly realized it was mostly aimed at the immediate vicinity of where we were currently. So, I spoke to Rachel about attending a class in Pensacola, which would be closer to where we were looking to relocate. So, in August of 2014, Rachel and I flew to Pensacola and attended the workshop together. She learned everything I did, and I was able to absorb even more the second time around. This time, though, I was also able to network more successfully.

Now, with everything out of the way, all that was left was involving the higher-ups in my retirement, which I did a couple of days after talking to Rachel; my retirement ceremony was held in May 2015. It wasn't anything grand, just an intimate ceremony with my close family members, as well as my superiors and some of my team members who were a part of my squadron.

Twenty years of service, and Rachel was the one who helped me cross the finish line. We didn't know where we were going yet, but we were going together.

The ceremony began with an introduction by my Mom, followed by my retirement speech. I made sure it was not that sappy and emotional, but it was still a teary-eyed moment for me. Afterwards the speeches came and awards were presented to me by my peers. One key thing for me was involving the final, and probably most impactful Chief in my Chain and Command of that final tour, LSC Shawn Wimberly, or Wimbo as some called him. He helped me to grow more in the last year of my career because he wasn't showing favoritism towards myself or any of my peers. By treating me with that level of professional respect, he gave me the space to finish my twenty years with my head held high. I asked and he accepted, Wimbo gave the invocation and benediction for my career, something I felt was appropriate. And to end it, my family and friends who were there got me some gifts, and we celebrated my bittersweet farewell to a big chapter of my life.

The reason for the Redemption Tour. Retirement wasn't the end, just the beginning of being the father they deserved.

Even though I was technically cleared for retirement in May, my last official reporting date was set at the end of June. So, I technically still served till then, just on terminal leave, enjoying my last days in the Navy. And just like that, eventually, the day came when I was officially retired from the Navy.

My commanding officer and I at my retirement ceremony.

June had passed, and now I was on my own. No more waking up at the crack of dawn, staying up all night to work on test reports, reporting to my seniors at the end of the day, or worrying about members of my squadrons. I was now the master of my own fate. For the first time in twenty years, the world didn't feel too loud. The crickets were still there, but the pressure of the flight line and the duty sections was gone. I had the liberty to choose my own volume. I had been in the Navy since I was old enough to vote. I knew that there was no rush, but due to my time in the Navy, I had developed the habit of wanting to be productive for at least part of my day. I knew that I'd go senile if I just sat around all day, lounging around, doing nothing.

Prior to retirement, my attempts to find a job involved Bradley Morris, a headhunting company known to assist military veterans who are trying to integrate once again into society and find work to help their transition. According to the company's standard of procedure, each veteran was assigned a specific mentor, if you will, who was responsible for utilizing the company network. After that, he would find work across the country to best suit the veteran, and my guy presented me with opportunities that were pretty good. The pay was more than enough, and the areas were all desirable as well, but the issue was that none of the places he took us to had what we were looking for. We had settled on the Panhandle of Florida.

Another issue was that, although he was good at what he did, the same could not be said about his personality. Rachel and I had already mentioned to him that we were looking for something in Florida, but he seemed to come to me with work everywhere except that place. I was already looking on my own, going to career fairs a couple of days a week, looking and hunting. I had a few interviews and a couple of offers. But the best was when I was offered my first job from a company called Nordco as a non-destructive inspector on rails. I had to decline when I learned I would be away from home as much as the Navy had done for me.

The Bradley Morris rep I was assigned, kept throwing worse and worse potential places for us to relocate to. It reached a point where I was absolutely done with his behavior. Enraged, I informed him that we could not continue with him if he was not able to get me what I wanted. What was surprising was that instead of being more lenient, he doubled down, rudely replying that it was impossible for me to find a job with the income I was looking for in the Florida Panhandle, which was only $50k a year. I figured that was fair enough to start with all of my experience. This was my limit, and it absolutely infuriated me. After that interaction, I knew that he was not looking out for my best interests, and I let go of him immediately.

I continued to apply to places, and even though I received a number of offers, I had to turn down most of them. I wish I could have accepted, but there were too many negatives. Some posts required me to spend most of my time away from my family, which beat the purpose of retirement, while others did not offer that much pay or were not even near Florida. I had to keep attending job fairs during my last year in the Navy, even buying a suit to make a good impression at the fairs. Although it was possible, the probability of your dream job offer landing in your lap right there at the fair was incredibly low, and I didn't expect one either. The main reason I invested in a suit and went to job fairs was for networking purposes. Other than networking at job fairs, that TAP class from August of 2014 had bumped up the possibility of getting the type of job I wanted. That class in Pensacola did wonders for me, as I got acquainted with someone there who handed me his business card.

Other than that, we also looked up potential neighborhoods we could settle in, deciding on the best area to eventually buy our house.

All of the time and money we invested in this pathway bore fruit once we retired and went to Florida. Upon returning, we first visited the Hurlburt Air Force Base to acquire our retired military IDs. While there, we also decided to pay a visit to the guy whom we met at that TAP class back in August. He was a lot of help. This time around, he handed us a list of companies better than the listings the headhunting company offered. After looking, I shortlisted four of them as they had potential for growth: Waffle House Manager, FAA Helpdesk technician for L3 Security Systems, Boeing, and AT&T wireless sales.

In an effort to secure a job, I reached out to them for an interview as soon as possible, hoping for the best-case scenario. After a few phone calls, it appeared that Boeing didn't show any real interest at the time. All the other companies were incredibly eager to further discuss employment with me. So, there I was, phone to my ear, attempting to sound confident through every call. I remember sitting in the Walmart parking lot; although I was trying to sound confident, deep down, I was desperate and willing to jump on the first offer I got.

L3 was the first to offer me something concrete, and while it wasn't exactly glamorous, it was something. I took the job at almost $40k a year without a second thought. I knew I was starting from the bottom again, and pride wasn't going to pay the bills. It was a stepping stone, and that's how I treated it. I ended up working with L3 for two months, just long enough to get my bearings, when The Boeing Company actually circled back. Out of nowhere, I got an offer I couldn't refuse, it was my dream job. When Boeing finally called back, it was the start of the career I had actually been preparing for during all those late nights on the flight line. With more growth potential ahead, I didn't hesitate. I left L3 on good terms, packed up what we had, and made the jump.

We stayed at my mom's and Curt's place in Andalusia, Alabama, while everything transitioned. They had just moved back down from Milwaukee for her work, and she was lucky enough to be doing it from home now, with the occasional international travel. That house became a bit of a landing pad for us, somewhere stable while we figured out our next move. We finally closed on our own place in November of 2015, and that made everything feel real.

It's funny to think back on what the headhunter told me, how I'd never get the kind of salary I wanted in Florida. I still think about that sometimes, how quickly people are to assume what's possible for you. He didn't know me. He didn't know what I was willing to do or how hard I'd work. I got what I aimed for, and today, I make a great deal more than what I made at L3. Every goal I've set, I've hit. Not because it was easy, but because I refused to settle for someone else's limits. The life I envisioned for my family in the Florida Panhandle is alive and thriving, exactly where we want to be.

Chapter 23
A New Beginning, Again?

It's weird, following a particular schedule your entire life, only for everything to end one day. I had gotten so used to the lifestyle that I had developed while in the Navy that when I retired, I suddenly didn't know what to do. There was no Morning or Evening Colors at 0800 every day, something the U.S. Navy adopted from the Royal Navy back in 1843. There was no more being told on short notice that there was a detachment or workups for deployment. You might think that I would be celebrating not being told what to do 24 hours a day, 7 days a week, and honestly, I thought so as well.

However, when you are integrated into a system for 20 plus years of your life, it becomes a part of you, for better or worse, and when that is taken away, no matter how strenuous or unfair it was, it leaves you hollow. You suddenly feel like you're left on your own, and your new way of life definitely takes some getting used to. It did for me at least. Life suddenly became uncertain, nothing was a gimme anymore, not the three square meals a day, a roof over my head, the paychecks on the 1st and the 15th of every month without fail.

I remember that there were days right after retiring when I used to wake up at my usual time while I was in service with the Navy, and would begin looking for my uniform without any other thought in my mind. Even though, luckily, I was easily able to adjust to my new life in a couple of months, I feel like there were some things that the Navy had hardwired into my mind that I took more time than I should have to let go. There were some serious moments of depression, moments in which I doubted my abilities.

Other than adjusting to a new routine, my emotions were subconsciously holding me back as well. All of my life, from when I turned 18, my only constant was working in the Navy; hell, even before joining the Navy, there was not much constant, and it was scary starting again from scratch with the added pressure of being the primary income for my family, especially at this point in my life. I knew that even with all of my experience I had gained over the last 20 years, I was going to have to swallow my pride and start again from the bottom.

That thought kept me up for many nights, but when I began dividing up my plan into different phases with different, achievable goals, something the Navy taught me, my mind was more at ease. In Naval Aviation, we had scheduled intervals for all kinds of maintenance, and this was how I was trying to think. When I reviewed the master plan that Rachel and I built together, I realized that the road to success is long but not impossible. I would just have to do my very best, no more fucking up like the first half of my Navy career, so basically, what I had been doing the second half of my career.

Once I put all my scattered thoughts on paper and came

up with a plan, it was time to put it into action. In my new career, I was responsible for writing technical manuals that the maintainers would use to perform work on specific parts of the plane. An instruction that would carefully explain each process from its maintenance to repair. This was a big deal to me as I used those very same manuals myself as a maintainer on helicopters.

They are what keep that aircraft in the air; people's lives depend on how accurately those manuals are written. One wrong word in the wrong place changes the entire context of a maintenance step and could mean that someone leaves a bolt uninstalled when it should have been installed.

For any average person starting out working in this role, all this documentation and the jargon may seem incredibly complicated and mind-numbing. However, I had just retired from being an avionics technician in the Navy, which involved performing aircraft electrical and electronic repairs and maintenance, which is why I more or less had an idea about the workflow and basic functionalities of pretty much any aircraft. But in the Navy, I was technically hands-on since I was the one working on the aircraft, whereas in my new job, I was supporting those that were serving in my place now, which was a very different perspective. The best part was that I could still serve my country through my new career after the Navy.

Nonetheless, I knew I had an advantage and used my avionics knowledge as a launchpad in order to boost the quality of the documents I wrote, and it worked. My manager was happy with my work ethic, and it showed in the roles and responsibilities placed on me in looking for ways to improve our quality. I was able to identify inefficiencies from the first day, even if my quality was not initially great due to the lack of initial training. This was something that nearly cut my career short before ever getting off the ground.

Still, I was happy this new career was allowing me plenty of time to spend with my family. And I would eventually learn my new environment and accelerate my performance. In the beginning, even my peers would recognize my potential; some of them said they would be working for me one day.

Even though my previous knowledge really helped uplift my work, another great contributor to it was Rachel. She was, has, and will always be a pillar to me, always standing tall and supportive. She was there for me when I was not getting any work, and she was with me while I was working for the Navy, always going above and beyond for my sake. I remember that a few months had gone by with me working and writing the Navy publications, and when the time came, it was largely because of Rachel's support that I performed so well for my annual reviews and was able to qualify for my first annual bonus.

With Rachel's support combined with my background, work was going smoothly, but I knew that this was not my ultimate goal. I want to position myself in management so I can have a greater impact on change and improving the company. I told my hiring manager after I accepted the offer that I wanted to do 20 years with the company, just like I did with the Navy. However, there were many obstacles in my way that I had to plan to maneuver around if I could fulfill this goal, with one of the major roadblocks being deciphering the complexities of the business.

I was hitting roadblocks for quite a while, and it wasn't until I reviewed some of my work that I came up with ideas here and there. I started noticing little inefficiencies, the kind that most people overlook because they seem too small to matter. But I knew better. I had spent enough time working with processes and people to recognize how quickly small things could snowball into massive expenses. So, I started fixing what I could quietly. I came up with improvements to workflows and systems that ended up saving the company serious money, hundreds of thousands on one program, and even more on another. I never looked at these ideas as business ventures at the time. I just wanted to make things better, smoother, and more efficient. That mindset became my strength.

It was never about getting credit, either. I simply saw waste and could not ignore it. I don't talk much about the specifics because of the proprietary nature of the work, but I can say that I developed a way to shave off time from repeatable tasks across departments, changes that freed up hours each week and, when multiplied across teams and months, led to significant financial gains.

Eventually, I got pulled into a major effort in St. Louis. Leadership handpicked me to help organize, rewrite, and baseline their core processes. They wanted someone who could see the gaps and find a better path forward, and they trusted me with that challenge. I laid out a plan, pitched it, and now, for the last two years, I have been the one driving that initiative forward. Recently, in 2025, that initiative has caught the attention of more senior managers, and they continue to support it, and it has even branched off into another initiative, the creation of a continuous improvement team just for maintaining processes.

It was always funny to me how our company builds and maintains publications for customers around the world, and we do a great job at it, but some of our own processes were falling to the wayside. All of this made me realize something. I enjoy this kind of work, the part where you get to step back, look at how things are done, and then figure out how to do it smarter. It's where I thrive. That is why my long-term goal, if it isn't management, will be to eventually become a mentor to other likeminded people to uncover those same inefficiencies and guide them toward saving money by working smarter. But to get there, I know I must finish what I started. Going back to my time on that wooden deck of the same battleship my paternal grandpa served on in World War II, a legacy coming full circle, I am currently working toward my bachelor's degree at the University of Alabama. Every step I take is laying the foundation for that next chapter, building on what he started decades ago.

My temporal journey, through my family's history, my grandpa's time in WWII, Grandma's survival in that same war as a child, all of the moments learning about their history, was coming full circle.

Chapter 24
Full Circle

After retiring from the Navy, the next step was to secure a job, and after asking around, giving nerve-wracking interviews, and anxiously waiting for calls, and received some rejections from the companies I was aiming for. I was reluctant to apply to other places since they did not fit what I was looking for.

So, defeated, I decided to accept the job I had been offered with L3 as a helpdesk technician because pride doesn't pay the bills, but I kept my eyes on my financial goals. However, during my training period with L3, fate had other plans as I received a call from a company that set the standards for aerospace, and I had to jump on the offer. I was around eight weeks into my training, when I got a call from their HR department, and not only did they offer me the position of technical writer that I initially wanted, but the annual salary was exactly $10,000 more than my current situation at the time, so I was ecstatic.

I had finally secured the job that fit all the requirements I was looking for, and I was determined to grow even further. However, just because I got hired didn't mean that life was all figured out. In fact, a new journey had just begun, but I was excited and equally determined to outperform my peers and go up the corporate ladder one promotion at a time.

I was hired as a level 1 technical data designer, which was the lowest designation, and my job description required me to write publications on F/A-18 jets, which was easier said than done. Even though I did have experience working with technical publications prior to retirement, I had exclusively worked on helicopters, so this was a relatively new experience for me.

My lack of knowledge about jets and their specifications, and intermittent training at best, along with the 6-month delay between my submitted work and the critical feedback on it, made the start of my new career rocky. However, I had always been a fast learner and was quick to adapt to a new environment.

Soon enough, my hard work began paying off. As time went by, I absorbed information like a sponge and polished my technical writing skills with each passing day, and with that, I was able to get past the slump of lacking knowledge about jets, and it wasn't until a particular project that my performance was also being noticed by other employees and managers as well.

On my team locally, there was no one above level 3, most of those level raises were on another team located in St. Louis. There was something that stuck with me, one of the guys training me said *"We'll be working for you one day."* I was flattered, but I was still learning and wasn't there, yet, not even close.

During that time, a particularly difficult publication project had landed on our desks. It was just the beginning of my employment, so I was still figuring out how to improve the quality of publications produced during that time, and this assignment was not only very complex, but the fact that none of my team members had any experience with it made this even more difficult. The quality of work I produced had been mediocre at best, which is why, at one point, the team discussed removing me. I faced hot water, and my career hung by a thread until my local manager rescued me with a suggestion and the advice of my eventual mentor, Ray.

He had kept an eye on me from the very beginning and saw the potential in me. I learned nearly 9 years later, that he spoke with my manager about putting me on a team where I could thrive, so I was switched over to another team that needed bodies on it, one I had relatable experience for. My manager had helped me this time, but he didn't let me off that easily. After transferring over to the team, I was to be put on probation until I showed visible improvement in my performance. Thankfully, that probation was what I needed, as it allowed me time to work on myself, and before I knew it, just a couple of months later, I had polished myself to the point that I was teaching advanced technical data designing and writing in front of the same people who trained me when I was first hired.

It wasn't long before I was recognized as a subject matter expert. That might sound like a big title for someone fresh into the job, but it came with the grind. I spent long days and longer nights learning, asking questions, fixing problems. My new manager noticed. He moved me into my own office space with eight desks. Any new hires or new team members came through my door first. I was responsible for getting them up to speed before they went solo. That trust meant a lot to me.

But the climb wasn't without its hits. I remember interviewing for a Level 2 job with my manager, thinking I was ready. I had done the work, earned the experience, but he passed me over. The job went to someone who never even joined our team. That hurt. It jaded me a little. But instead of letting it get the best of me, I used it. I stayed focused. I got better.

Not long after, I was asked to travel to Philadelphia. Our program was struggling, and they needed a small group of us to figure out what was going wrong. I was one of the few handpicked to go. I interviewed for a Level 2 job on another team and was offered the position. That manager was someone I had met in a transition class when I was retiring from the Navy. He was the very first person I had ever talked to from the company, before I even applied. It felt like the right move. So, I took it.

That was September 2018. Exactly 34 months after I started, I hit Level 2. A year later, in September 2019, I applied for a Level 3 job back in Philly. I had met someone while traveling there earlier, and the opportunity opened up. I told my current manager about it, and to my surprise, he countered me with the same offer to keep me on the team. I accepted. Two promotions in two years. I was moving fast. But I wasn't chasing the title. I was chasing impact and results.

I got to work on two brand new projects we had just landed. One was a new helicopter for the Air Force. The other was a new tanker drone for the Navy. Both are high-profile, complex, and demanding. I dove in headfirst, again teaching myself new systems and finding better ways to do things. I became the program focal and a go-to SME. My peers had degrees. Some had a Master's. I had none of that, not yet. But I had experience, and I had results.

Five and a half years into my new journey, my team lead retired. I applied for his job. It was a long shot. But I got it. That was May 2021. I hit Level 4 in under six years, with no degree. It was my proudest professional achievement, a personal goal. And it all happened while I was still working toward my degree. Right in the middle of the pandemic.

Now I was leading the very teams I had helped build. I continued working with the Navy on drone development. Every year, I asked for performance feedback from our Navy customer and from my peers. And every year, the feedback was glowing. I had built strong relationships with the customer, so strong that at one point, the Navy tried to hire me away from my current position. The catch? I would have had to move to Patuxent River, Maryland. But my wife didn't want that. And I didn't want to uproot our lives again.

Eventually, our Navy program began to struggle, not because of the work we were doing, but because senior program managers had set it up poorly from the start. An outside team was brought in to audit and help us course correct. A team from Philly eventually took over. I had no say in it, but I didn't sulk. I trained the new team myself. I showed them how to do my job and ensured the handoff was clean.

During that transition, I was asked to become a process focal for both our local area and the wider enterprise. I joined a small team of eight who traveled every few months to assess and improve processes across different business units. I also earned a reputation as the guy who could fix broken systems. When a special project needed someone to step in and turn it around, I got the call.

A senior manager in St. Louis approached me with a unique scenario. They wanted me to review the processes for the entire Fighter Jet division. That was the same department I had started in years ago, the one that almost got me fired due to poor training and outdated systems. It felt like everything had come full circle. Now, I was the one fixing what had once nearly derailed my career.

I facilitated meetings, coordinated with managers across departments, and led teams through the schedule I had built from scratch, without a degree, through hard work and a relentless drive to improve. And in 2024, I was asked to become a Quality Technical Lead Engineer, a TLE, a key leadership role across the enterprise. That was nearly nine years from when I first walked in the door.

Of course, the road wasn't smooth. In the beginning, I almost lost my job. The processes were outdated, the training insufficient, and there was no clear guidance for someone like me. I felt lost. The biggest challenge was convincing leadership that we needed change. I could have quit. I could have taken the easy way out, as others did. I saw people around me complain endlessly about how they got screwed, about how the system never changes. But none of them had faced what I had. None of them had nearly been fired.

That experience gave me perspective. I used it as fuel. Every challenge became a stepping stone, and I poured that frustration into doing better, providing more for my family, and making my workplace better than how I found it.

That is what I tell people now when they come to me, unsure of their path. Do not wallow in defeat. Do not wait for things to magically improve. Be the one who improves them. Show your value. Earn your spot.

That belief came from watching the people who raised me. My grandma. My mom. My dad. My mom started on a forklift. She didn't even have a high school diploma. Just a GED. But she climbed, and she climbed far. By the time she retired, she was a regional manager in a global company. She led teams in Chile, Australia, Canada, and across the United States. She built a retirement that now sits higher than most Americans. My dad, the man who raised me, worked offshore in the oil industry. He topped out at very well-paid salary every year as a rig manager, again with only a high school education. He taught me what it meant to work hard. To do things for others, not just for money, but because it was right.

He had me mow lawns for our elderly neighbors. Sometimes he made me do it for free. He said, "Because it's the right thing to do." That stuck with me. I never forgot that lesson.

So, when I talk to other veterans, other retirees trying to find their place again, I tell them this: do not chase the biggest paycheck. Do not jump at the first company offering more money. Go where you are valued. Go where you can grow. You may start lower than others, but if the company sees your worth and invests in you, that is worth more than any short-term raise.

I had friends who chased the bigger paychecks. They got more up front. But they never moved up. They never got the chance to lead, to change anything. I did. I earned back-to-back promotions, I led two teams, and I helped steer national defense programs. I got asked to join strategic improvement groups. And I am not done yet.

In the next two to three years, I will finish my degree. And when that day comes, I plan to push for higher roles because I know I can do it, especially once I get my degree.

This chapter of my life has been about more than just proving people wrong. It has been about proving to myself that I am capable of more than I ever thought. That with the right work ethic, the right attitude, and the right heart, you can rise from anywhere to anywhere. That is what acing it looks like to me.

Chapter 25
Finding Lost Links

After years of struggling, first in the Navy and then after retirement, making money and establishing myself at the place I wanted, life was finally how I had envisioned it to be. I had a loving wife and children who were the light at the end of the tunnel. I finally had everything I wanted. Except that was not true, as one thought still haunted my nights: family.

You see, my dad, who had raised me, was not really my biological father. He adopted me the day I was born, though I didn't discover the truth until I was 16. Until then, I thought he was my biological father, but even after that revelation, he was always and still is my dad. At that time, it felt as if my life had been a lie up until that point, but nonetheless, I found a way to come to terms with it, not because I had processed the idea, but rather duc to the fact that I did not have the means as a 16-year-old to go on a wild goose chase to find my real dad.

As the years passed, I had time to process that idea, my mind wandered elsewhere, and from there on, I started wondering about my biological father. Ever since finding the truth, I was curious. *What did he look like? What would his reaction be if he saw me? Is he even alive?* Oftentimes, I used to zone out into the distance, thinking about it.

You might think that as time went by, the curiosity would eventually fade away, but it was quite the opposite. As time went by and I got older, I grew even more curious, which my dad often fueled, when he would say things like, "You have good genes, your grandpa is still strong at 90 years old." It didn't really anger me when he said stuff like that, but it did bother me because he and I both knew that my grandfather was not the one responsible for my genes.

As my age crept up on me and I realized I was not as indestructible as my behavior reflected, I realized that there are certain health concerns my father could pass down. All this time, it was not that I only wanted to find out if I had a whole other family out there, but, more importantly, because I needed to better understand where I came from genetically.

One of the first times holding my new granddaughter after she was born.

It is one of those things where some people don't think about it until it is too late, but I now have a granddaughter as well as my three daughters to think about. It was the responsible thing to at least consider these questions.

This urge to find and connect with my bio-father only grew with the years. I knew that it was not going to be easy. So, with that in mind, I decided to contact detectives and other agencies, using the connections I made in the Navy as a recruiter, to gather information on whether he was still alive or not. As the search had continued, I had never realized it was truly getting under my skin, until I got a call… It felt as if I had been holding a breath all this time, which I only released when they informed me that they were unable to find anything on the little information I had given them from when I was 16.

Rachel had an excellent idea: Let's use genetic testing through two of the most prominent players in the industry, 23andMe and Ancestry, for Christmas in 2017. I followed the directions for both and shipped them off, waiting for results, which would come in March of 2018. I had a map of my genetics, half of which was known to me, my maternal side.

This would make the search much easier once I identified known relatives on Mom's side. I had some I suspected on her side, but wasn't sure, until I found out that my cousin John John was also in the system. This made it so easy, I could mark everyone we had as common connections as my maternal side, so everyone else by default was on my bio-father's side. The search wasn't as easy as hoped, though.

I had helped my cousin find out he had a half-sister that he never even knew he had or had a reason to suspect, but I was still looking for my biological father. It was more than four years later, in August 2022, when I had been putting puzzle pieces together, thinking I was getting closer to thinking my biological surname was Nesbitt, when I learned it was more likely to be Stanard. But it wasn't my father I had found; it appeared to be a sibling based on the centimorgans, or simply put, a unit of measure to show how close or distant a relative is using genetic markers.

When I found this final clue, I was ecstatic to say the least. It felt as if this broken and rusty chain in my mind was reforming. Hope and happiness filled my heart, where a gaping void had once formed after the death of my supposedly only blood sibling, Roy. I thought he was the only blood brother I had, but I was glad that I was wrong. Now that I had some information on my new brother's existence, what I didn't have was how to get in touch with him. That made the search even more obsessive. I sent a message in the system even though it showed he hadn't been online for a while.

Eventually, by the end of August, we connected. We both had been on each other's trail. He had also been looking because he wondered if he had any other relatives out there. We started messaging back and forth, feeling out the situation, making sure it was real. His name is Scott Stanard. We finally got comfortable enough, we exchanged phone numbers and set up a time to call.

As the phone rang, my heart pounded with anticipation, nervousness, and fear. Many thoughts were bubbling in my mind, wondering if this was the right thing to do. What if he knew about me all this time but did not reach out to me intentionally? However, when he picked up the call, all those thoughts were put to rest.

He was just as happy as I was when we talked for the first time, maybe a little more than I was initially, since I was still looking for a father, but I was still happy. There were no awkward pauses, hostility, or negative emotions, just love between two brothers whom circumstances had separated, but who finally reunited. We connected right away, updating each other on what we both had been doing all these years, talking and laughing as if we had known each other all our lives. However, as they say, both sides of a coin have to balance each other out, and just like a coin, accompanied by such great events came unfortunate news as well.

As we were talking on the phone, I enthusiastically suggested meeting up, but he refused. At first, I thought that I might have jumped the gun; after all, this was literally the first conversation we were having. However, what he told me was much grimmer. He had been diagnosed with kidney failure some time ago, so some days after his treatments, he couldn't get out of bed, let alone travel somewhere. This was mainly because of the dialysis scheduled three days a week, and then also because he lived in Alaska. The news hit me like a ton of bricks, and I was devastated that my little brother was going through such pain.

I had already lost one brother, and now it seemed inevitable that I could lose the one I just found. Nevertheless, I didn't let this ruin the connection we both made. I took it upon myself to stay in contact with him despite the distance we couldn't travel. I would call and text him often. He was working for a company that built asphalt surfaces for a military base in Alaska, so we would chat on his breaks sometimes. As we got into the holidays, we even set up a FaceTime call on Christmas morning, where he met Rachel and talked to his nieces for the first time.

On that day, that morning, watching him make my usually shy daughters laugh and cackle and get along with my wife made my heart flutter. It just seemed easy and effortless. That day, everything felt right, and it felt like a Christmas miracle. Unfortunately, as much as I wanted to be there for him during his dialysis, he lived in Alaska, so I couldn't be of much help. However, I made sure to keep in touch with him, calling him whenever I got time to check up on him, letting him know that I was just one call or text away. That was almost three years ago.

We are still closely connected today. You would be happy to know that we even met up for the first time in person recently. His mom, Inez, lives in Mesa, Arizona. He decided he was moving there for a better chance at getting a kidney, and his mom would be there to help him out, also. I was not aware he was getting ready to move, though; somehow it never made it into conversation until I told him I was going on a work trip to one of our facilities in Mesa. The crazy part is how he was flying down the same week I was going to be there, which also happened to be the week of my 48th birthday in April 2024. People say it's a crazy coincidence, but I'd like to think that it's the strings of fate doing a solid for me for once. You couldn't make this stuff up.

Since I was attending meetings all week, I had arranged to stay two days longer through the weekend instead of flying back home on Friday. Scott and I met in person on Friday, the day after my birthday.

Lunch with Scott after meeting my "new" brother for the first time in Scottsdale.

He came and picked me up at my hotel, and we rode around, winding up in Scottsdale. We found a little restaurant called the Montauk, where we sat and had breakfast and chatted for a while. We told our server our story, because why not? It's an awesome story, and we wanted to share it with her. She thought it was one of the coolest stories she had heard and was so thankful that she was basically a part of our story. After breakfast, we wandered around all day, with Scott showing me the sights in and around Scottsdale and Old Town Scottsdale.

As I sit here, I realize that life has the nasty habit of throwing you a doozy every once in a while, and oftentimes, not in a good way. Whether it was my divorce from Erin, my mistake of not fighting harder and sooner for Kathleen when she was a baby, or Roy's death, it's safe to say that my life has not exactly been all smooth sailing. However, I realize that the bumpier the ride, the more scenic the destination. But I also look back to grandma and my mom, and their lives. My bumps along the way were all possible because they survived, they endured much harder things that hopefully I will never have to deal with. And all those downs in life? They are opportunities to learn and be a better person, rather than something to wallow over your entire life.

Although parts of my life did cause me a lot of emotional and physical pain at times, I can positively say that if I hadn't gotten back up every time life beat me down, and instead wallowed over all my past blunders without doing anything about them, I would never have become the man I am today. It is, after all, these tests that shape your life to be the one you wish for. And what I wish for?

Even with crickets in my head a constant reminder of my time in the Navy, I find peace in the moments that matter the most, whether it is one of the rare occasions I get to hold my granddaughter, the first time I got to have breakfast with my newfound brother Scott, or the gift of witnessing those everyday moments with Ava and Everly that I missed out on with Kathleen, there is a newfound silence with the life I have built through the struggles.

Many people wish for immense riches or fame at the end of their lives, but to me, this was it. A roof to call home, my beautiful children and loving wife that know I am here to stay, a granddaughter, and a brother found. To me, this isn't just the dream, it is a *legacy unbroken* because of my grandmother's survival.

I have witnessed people in my life who succumb to their failures instead of getting back up and learning from them. Some people must fight harder than others to get past obstacles, but there are people who don't walk away from that fight, while others fold. I would never suggest that one person's challenge is more meaningful than another's. What I will say is that some people have more fight in them. Their will to survive and endure the challenges they face is what makes life more meaningful.

Some people would say the world is against them, but do you think those people who surrounded my four-year-old Grandma in a Japanese intern camp thought that? I can tell you from stories I heard that most of them did not feel that. They survived because they had hope. Their hope is the equivalent of why so many generations of families around the world even exist today. It's the reason people around the world have endured for thousands of years. It's my reason for writing this book, my reason I am a son, my reason I am a husband, my reason I am a father and grandfather, and probably the foundation of it all, it's my reason for living. What are the reasons you, your family, your friends, your neighbors; what are the reasons we are all here?

Grandma's life, it's the memories she shared, lessons she learned, photographs she showed me, all echoes through time, all showing me why we are here. As I consider these reasons, I realize Grandma is the reason for my existence, but I am also reminded that the actions of American soldiers and Filipino guerrillas in a world at war are why I am here - why we are all still here. For that reason, I walked my daughter Kathleen down the aisle for her wedding on November 15, 2025.

Today, I am afraid, and I wonder: Are there still people like that? I like to think there are, and I must hope there are, so that my granddaughter and her future family can keep the echoes of Los Baños reverberating. It is Grandma's survival and the soldiers' and guerrillas' bravery during a daring rescue that allows me to be here, a legacy that extends 87 years across time.

This is how we remember; this is how our legacies remain unbroken.

Acknowledgment

While the foundation of this book starts with her, I still must take a moment to briefly acknowledge Grandma. The rest of my acknowledgements are going to be chronological, but I need to thank my brother, "Roy Boy," up front; he was my first test in life for what it truly means to experience loss.

I want to give credit to Mom, Dad, and Curt for being there for me as a kid into adulthood. Thank you for not only supporting the example that I saw in Grandma, but also setting your own examples. You all showed me what hard work can do, not for the sake of appearance, but from the inner satisfaction and drive that comes from a life well lived. For the nurturing, the tough love, and yes, even the embarrassing moments, thank you.

Growing up in that small town of Florala, Alabama, was a beautiful part of my life. Yet, it wasn't until I was forced away that I really saw the world as I needed to see it, how Grandma saw it: Big, wide open, and full of diversity. While I admire those who can stay in one place their entire lives, I don't know that my journey would have brought me to where I am now had I never left.

This brings me to the next major point in my journey, and the most special thank you of all, to the love of my life, my beautiful wife, Rachel. It has been your unwavering support and love that have allowed me to arrive at this specific moment in time, typing the acknowledgements for my first book. It was that love that brought into this world our two beautiful, vibrant daughters, Ava and Everly. Thank you to my girls for helping me continue to grow. I may not always be the best Daddy I could be, but you certainly keep me honest. And of course, I can't forget my wonderful mother-in-law, Teresa. Thank you for raising such a wonderful daughter for me to discover and spend the rest of my life with.

I can't give thanks to my oldest daughter, Kathleen, without giving thanks to her mother, my ex-wife, Erin. You raised our beautiful daughter alongside a man whom I have the utmost respect for, Dom. So, thank you, Kathleen, Erin, and Dom, for your continuous support from my time in the Navy to where we are today. Seeing you, Kathleen, get married this year was a blessing because of that support.

My wider circle of family and friends, please know that if you are reading this, I appreciate the role you played in my life. I do, however, have to thank a few people who provided invaluable practical support on this project. Thank you to my cousin, Kim Lawson, and an old Navy buddy, Mike Barger, for taking the time to proofread and provide necessary feedback. Finally, thank you to the Book Writing Cube's editing team for your work on this year-long project.

www.ingramcontent.com/pod-product-compliance
Lightning Source LLC
LaVergne TN
LVHW100521110826
845146LV00002B/734

9798994964903